Scotland to the World

National
Museums
Scotland

Scotland to the World
Treasures from the National Museum of Scotland

Published in 2016 by
NMS Enterprises Limited – Publishing
a division of NMS Enterprises Limited
National Museums Scotland
Chambers Street
Edinburgh EH1 1JF
www.nms.ac.uk

Publication edited by David Souden, Past Present Ltd
with Catherine Holden and Xerxes Mazda

ISBN 978 1 910682 05 0

Designed by Mark Blackadder

Cover images: Cover illustrations (left to right): Top row: National Museum of
Scotland Tower entrance (© Sean Bell Photography); Water jar for tea ceremony;
Carved stone ball; *'Willowwood'* grand piano; Scottish Parliament commemor-
ative medal; Robert Wilson demonstration piece; African carved female figure;
CERN copper accelerating cavity; Lewis Chessmen king; Biting midge in amber;
Darien chest; National Museum of Scotland Grand Gallery. Bottom row: Giant
white butterfly from Dufresne Collection; Buddha sculpture; John Logie Baird
Televisor; Ballarat gold nugget; Ivory portrait medallion by David Le Marchand;
Susannite; Hunterston brooch; Dolly the sheep; Court mantua; *Piper to the Laird
of Grant*; Arthur Seat coffins; Ancient Greek *lekythos*. (Unless otherwise stated,
© National Museums Scotland)

Image on page vi © Andrew Lee

For a full listing of NMS Enterprises Limited – Publishing titles and related
merchandise: www.nms.ac.uk/books

SHEPHERD+ WEDDERBURN

This publication is supported by Shepherd and Wedderburn

BELL
& BAIN
LIMITED

Printed and bound in the United Kingdom by
Bell & Bain Limited, Glasgow

Contents

Scotland to the World

Foreword

Dr Gordon Rintoul CBE
Director, National Museums Scotland

The collections of National Museums Scotland are one of the most diverse in any National Museum in the world. They bring together the arts and sciences, the cultures of Scotland and the world, and the full spectrum of human ingenuity and creativity alongside the diversity of the natural world. With deep roots, spanning thousands of years, they were gathered by explorers and adventurers, inventors and innovators, politicians and traders, historians and archaeologists, designers and naturalists. Our collections enable us to explore, to debate and to celebrate our nation and the world around us – past, present and future.

Amongst our four museums, the sheer breadth of our holdings is perhaps most powerfully seen in our largest site, the National Museum of Scotland. Located at the heart of Scotland's capital city, in its historic Old Town, this Museum has been the focus of nearly two decades of recent investment. This began with the 1998 extension that introduced the Scottish galleries, followed by the 2011 restoration of the building, with innovative displays of the natural world and world cultures,

then the 2016 opening of ten inspiring galleries of fashion, applied art and design, science and technology, and subsequently two new galleries of East Asia and Ancient Egypt. Thanks to the skills and dedication of our staff, the encouragement of many external advisers, and the support of many generous donors, this has been a historic transformation.

This book celebrates the extraordinarily rich collections showcased at the National Museum of Scotland, and is published on the occasion of its 150th anniversary. Opened in 1866 by HRH Prince Alfred, Duke of Edinburgh and son of Queen Victoria, the institution was inspired by the work of generations of pioneers and thinkers, and this publication honours their legacy.

I hope that readers will find much to engage, enthuse and inspire them. The production of the book has been supported by Shepherd and Wedderburn, and I would like to record my thanks to them for enabling the creation of such a handsome tribute.

Opposite: The Grand Gallery, featuring the Window on the World display.

The World to Edinburgh
The National Museum of Scotland through the ages

Henrietta Lidchi

The Museum which I have been commending to you is not a museum of Scottish Industry, but a museum of the world in relation to Scotland. It cannot be less than this …. To no one nation has been given the monopoly of genius, constructive skill or practical sagacity.

This visionary statement was delivered in 1857 by George Wilson, the first Director of what we now know as the National Museum of Scotland.

In the early 1850s, in that euphoric moment that followed the 1851 Great Exhibition in London, a campaign was launched for an Industrial Museum in Edinburgh. Founded by an Act of Parliament in 1854, it was the first national museum to be created outside London. George Wilson (1818–59) conceptualised the institution as one that would house exhibition spaces, a laboratory (or workshop), a library, and a programme of lectures to encourage intellectual access. Key to its success would be its collections. He invited correspondents across the globe, often Scots, to supply raw materials, intermediate stages and finished products, as well as tools, apparatuses and machines, all of which he believed both embodied ideas and demonstrated technological solutions. In 1855 Wilson was made the first (and only) Regius Chair of Technology at the University of Edinburgh; with a special remit for teaching the principles of industrial science, he worked to

Opposite: The Main Hall of the Edinburgh Museum of Science and Art, from the first floor balcony, by an unknown photographer, *c.*1867.

Above: Edinburgh-born George Wilson (1818–59), Professor of Technology at the University of Edinburgh and first Director of the Industrial Museum of Scotland.

promote the value of industrial museums in both public and scholarly circles. Although aspects of the Museum's role have predictably changed, his original emphasis on access, inspiration, ingenuity, progress and internationalism remain at its heart.

The current National Museum of Scotland has a history rooted not only in Wilson's pioneering Industrial Museum, but also in the University of Edinburgh's earlier Museum of Natural History, the former National Museum of Antiquities of Scotland, and the Royal Society of Edinburgh. All three were in existence by the early 19th century as collecting institutions ratified by Royal Charters. Broadly speaking each were heirs to the remarkable intellectual and scientific flourishing of the 18th-century Scottish Enlightenment, constituted to foster and promote curiosity, teaching and learning. Patronage, property and politics were the cultural context in which these academic and cultural institutions operated, as their fortunes waxed and waned.

The University of Edinburgh received its Royal Charter in 1582 and formed its initial collection from the latter part of the 17th century. In the early 19th century the newly-appointed Regius Professor of Natural History, Robert Jameson, began to build the collections, securing money from the Town Council and the Crown towards their upkeep. The University had by this time benefited from the collections of the Royal Society of Edinburgh, which were housed in the University museum (if natural history) or in the Library of the Faculty of Advocates (if antiquities).

In 1780 the Society of Antiquaries of Scotland was brought into being by its founder David Steuart Erskine, 11th Earl of Buchan, gaining a Royal Charter in 1783. Daniel Wilson, the brother of George Wilson, was Secretary and first cataloguer of its museum. Writing in 1849, he mischievously noted that the 'patriotic zeal' and 'personal exertions' that had characterised the Earl's collecting had not been equalled by his successors. The museum had an initial interest in antiquities and natural history, but an unwavering focus on archaeological material. The collections were gifted to the nation in 1851, passing into public ownership. Their location changed a number of times before settling into a purpose-built building on Queen Street in Edinburgh's New Town in the 1890s. Here the National Museum of Antiquities of Scotland shared a site for nearly a hundred years with the Scottish National Portrait Gallery, which remains there today.

For George Wilson, museums were philosophical endeavours which used architectural design as a key means to convey ideas. Prior to his untimely death in 1859, Wilson consistently argued for a bespoke building to house the grow-ing collection. Drawing up the plans fell to Captain Francis Fowke (1823–65), architect and engineer of, amongst other buildings, the Royal Albert Hall. Fowke designed the museum building in a Venetian Renaissance style and also evocative of

Left: Watercolour by Captain Francis Fowke (1823–65), architect and engineer of the building which opened in 1866 as the Edinburgh Museum of Science and Art; and an earlier design (opposite) for the interior of the Great Hall of the Industrial Museum of Scotland, signed by Fowke.

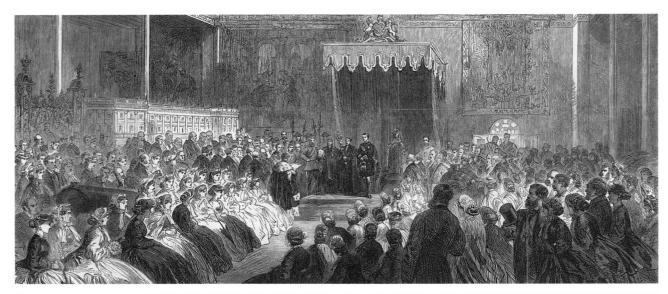

Above: HRH Prince Alfred, Duke of Edinburgh, opening the renamed Edinburgh Museum of Science and Art in 1866. Below: The eastern half of Chambers Street showing the Edinburgh Museum of Science and Art, a watercolour by David Cousin (with figures by Sam Bough).

Joseph Paxton's Crystal Palace, which housed the Great Exhibition of 1851. Plans were approved in 1861 and the foundation stone was laid by the champion of the Great Exhibition, HRH Prince Albert, husband of Queen Victoria. It was to be his last public duty before his death. The Department of Science and Art in London oversaw the completion of the first of three stages of work, which were supervised (after Fowke's own untimely death in 1865) by Scottish architect Robert Matheson (1808–77), the government's Clerk of Works for Scotland. The renamed Edinburgh Museum of Science and Art was opened in 1866 by Queen Victoria's son, HRH Prince Alfred, Duke of Edinburgh, to an enthusiastic reception. In its first full year, it welcomed more than a quarter of a million visitors.

Although as yet architecturally unfinished, the renamed museum showed a subtle shift in its focus and collecting practices. Wilson's successor, Thomas C Archer (1818–85), a botanist and civil servant who had supplied and catalogued botanical imports for the Great Exhibition, served as Director from 1859 to 1885. Archer preserved some of the early emphasis on technology and multi-disciplinary collections, actively bringing into the fold the University's Natural History collections. He frequently attended international exhibitions to make acquisitions for the Museum, and added personal gifts to enhance the collection. He is credited with expanding its scientific range, as well as developing an emphasis on the decorative arts, successfully securing donations and loans from manufacturing firms, developing small temporary exhibitions and introducing the idea of connoisseurship. Under Archer the Main Hall (now known as the Grand Gallery) was finished in 1875.

The third Director, from 1885 to 1900, was Sir Robert Murdoch Smith (1835–1900). Murdoch Smith was an archaeologist, diplomat and civil servant who had spent 20 years in Iran, from 1865 as Director of the Persian Telegraph Company which connected India to Great Britain. Multi-lingual, Murdoch Smith was appointed equally for his international connections as his fine administrative skills. Under his leadership the original Victorian architectural masterplan was completed, while he also increased the professional staff, oversaw the development

Directors Thomas C Archer (left) and Sir Robert Murdoch Smith (right).

of the collections and extended the public activities of the Museum. To mark the opening of the west wing in 1889, he invited the Shah of Iran, Nasir ad-Din, to visit. As reported in the *Scotsman,* 'His Majesty frequently expressed his admiration for Edinburgh … [and] remarked that the Scottish people seemed to him to have shown a wonderful amount of energy not only in their own country, but wherever they went'.

Any sense of intellectual or architectural completeness was inevitably momentary and the Museum continued to expand under a new generation of directors. Additions and architectural interventions were made throughout the 20th century, while the administrative oversight of the Museum passed from London to Edinburgh and the Scotch [*sic*] Education Department. In the 1930s building work revealed intact portions of the Flodden Wall (1513) which were preserved and revealed to the public. By the early 20th century curatorial activities were pursued in broadly four arenas: Natural Science, Geology, Technology, and Art and Ethnography, a model that proved largely relevant until the 1980s. The public galleries presented a dazzling array of objects, evolving across the decades, from fossils to furniture, Persian art to Scottish rocks, arms and armour to locomotives, medieval tapestries to Indian sculpture. New galleries added in the 1920s covered British Birds,

The hall in the east wing of the Edinburgh Museum of Science and Art, *c.*1890, showing the Natural History collections.

Comparative Ethnography and British Engineering. By 1938, the Museum was showing films on 18-inch screens to support its 'Native Art' galleries of Africa, Oceania and the Americas. A popular film of the Museum and its visitors was also made to show at the British Empire Exhibition in Glasgow.

In the early to mid-20th century the Royal Scottish Museum (as it was renamed) sought to affirm its role as a national museum, more actively reflecting aspects of Scottish industry, culture and crafts. This culminated in the landmark *Exhibition of Scottish Everyday Art* (1936), a temporary exhibition supported by craftsmen and manufacturers throughout Scotland and designed by the British modernist architect Sir Basil Spence (1907–76). The Museum perceived its national role as complementary to an international and scientific agenda that also saw it sponsor small fieldwork expeditions and collecting ventures. This enhanced definition of a national responsibility included providing professional assistance to local and regional museums, and secondments to national museums in London. Meanwhile the National Museum of Antiquities of Scotland decided on a narrower remit, primarily dedicated to the illustration of Scottish archaeology and history. In the 1930s it transferred on permanent loan all 'art objects' of non-Scottish provenance to the Royal Scottish Museum. This was converted into a gift in 1956.

Key to change in the 20th century was the Second World War, which saw the closure of the Museum for just under four years. The collections were moved, and the building was increasingly given over for a range of government functions including the Ministry of Health. This conceptual break initiated a sparer design of the galleries once they were reinstalled. Douglas Allan (1896–1967), Director between 1945 and 1961, reflected the post-war trend for reducing the number of cases in galleries and the number of objects in cases. Gone was the forest of plaster casts and sculpture in the Main Hall as it was turned over to a lively cycle of special exhibitions. During the 1950s and 1960s a series of modifications and modernist structures divided the space, hosting displays on such varied subjects as *Scottish Silver* (1950), *Hugh Miller* (1952), *African Art* (1956), *Design Today* (1956) and *Rocket Astronomy* (1960), to name but a few.

Over the 20th century, contemporary collecting, exchanges and transfers provided the institution with multiple historic collections. This was perhaps most fully cemented in 1985 with the amalgamation of the Royal Scottish Museum with the National Museum of Antiquities of Scotland. A striking modern wing was commissioned to house the Scottish collections, and this was opened in 1998 by HM The Queen. From 2004 attention was once again paid to the Victorian building, to ensure the glories of the original architecture were fully restored and the building made fit for 21st-century visitors. Collections held in storage behind the scenes were moved to the expanded National Museums Collection Centre in north Edinburgh. This permitted the creation of a street-level entrance hall, an enlarged special exhibition space, much improved public facilities and the transformation of the galleries. In 2011 two new suites of galleries were opened representing World Cultures and the Natural World. A vertical display, Window on the World, spanning three floors of the Grand Gallery, was created to celebrate the unique diversity of the Museum's holdings – a cabinet of curiosities for the 21st century which provides a spectacular glimpse of the wonders accumulated over two hundred years.

Today the organisation that is National Museums Scotland manages four museums, and cares for collections numbering over 12 million items. Arranged in five curatorial areas, these collections are celebrated by the publication of this book, which marks the 150th anniversary of the 1866 opening of the building now known as the National Museum of Scotland. To celebrate this historic occasion, two new suites of galleries have been opened, spanning European decorative arts, design and fashion alongside scientific and technological innovation. Bringing together art and science in this way honours the legacy of George Wilson's original vision, and the desire of generations of successive directors to build, research, preserve and interpret these extraordinarily diverse and fascinating collections for the benefit of all. Wilson argued a Museum should be 'for the public, with the public, by the public', and today the institution's ambition remains to inspire current and future generations through the treasures it holds, bringing Scotland to the attention of the world, and the world to Scotland.

Overleaf: The Grand Gallery today.

Window
on the world

Window
on the world

Scottish History and Archaeology

Our Scottish collections reflect the story of Scotland from the earliest times to the present day. They represent Scotland as a dynamically changing place, a sum of its many parts, shaped by networks of settlement, trade, travel and communication. They cover 15,000 years, alongside comparative material from Europe north of the Alps extending over 200,000 years.

The collections are internationally recognised as the essential resource for understanding Scotland's past. They are one of the most representative national collections of archaeological and historical artefacts anywhere in the world.

The Early Prehistory material includes finds from the iconic Neolithic village of Skara Brae in Orkney. The Iron Age, Roman and Early History collections contain masterpieces of early Celtic art, spectacular finds from the edge of the Roman world, and outstanding Early Medieval and Viking objects from the period when what became 'Scotland' began to emerge. Together, the Medieval, Early Modern and Late Modern collections trace the evolution of the Scottish kingdom and later developments in its history, as part of an imperial and post-imperial Britain.

Individual objects connect us to key people and events. The wide range of material, including decorative arts and social and military history, forms an unrivalled record of the life, times and achievements of Scotland's people at home and abroad.

The origin of the collections lies in material amassed by the Society of Antiquaries of Scotland founded in 1780 – the beginning of a systematic endeavour to preserve and understand Scotland's past. As today, the earliest collectors sought not only to research and record ancient artefacts, but also to encourage a wide appreciation of Scotland. Operating alongside their outward-looking scholarship was a patriotic endeavour to delineate a narrative where Scottish difference was recognised, valued and placed in its wider context. Within the collections there are many objects – a number of which are included in the following pages – which constitute national treasures; rare or unique survivals that are widely recognised as forming part of the fabric of Scotland's cultural inheritance.

Thanks to antiquarianism and chance finds, systematic archaeological excavation, targeted purchases, donations of treasured family possessions and dedicated efforts to collect the contemporary, the collections have developed over many generations. They are the precious material evidence from which changing ideas about Scotland – past, present and future – can be traced, constructed and shared.

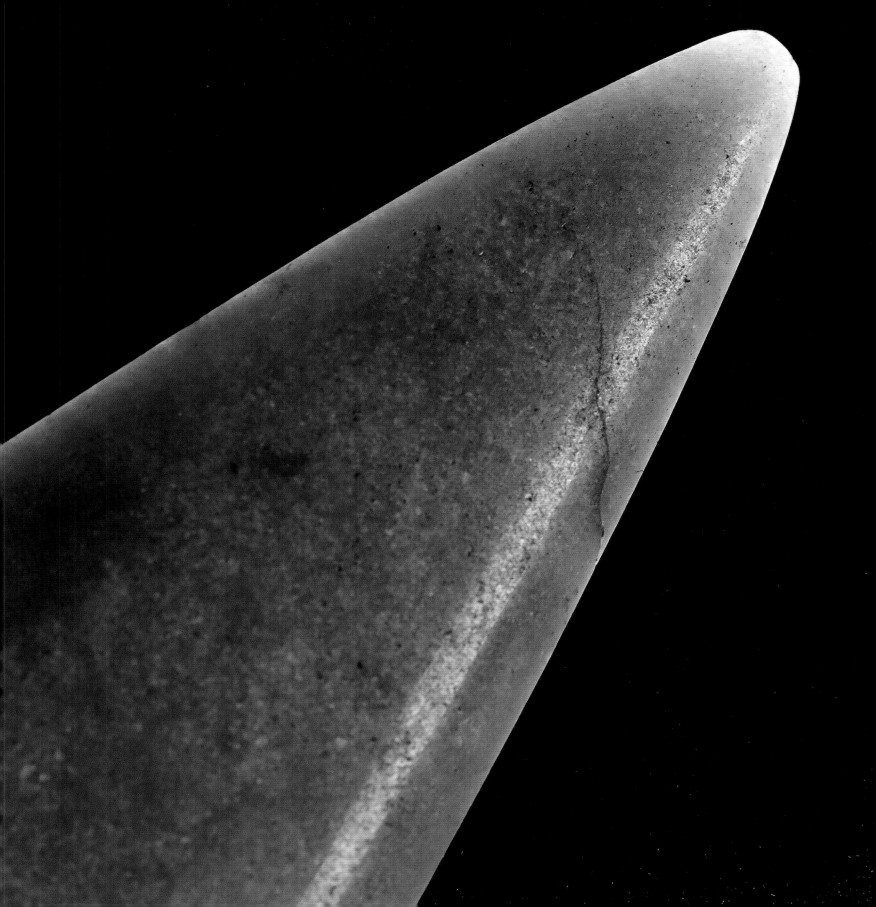

Mountain magic

This exquisite axehead, silky smooth and polished to a glassy sheen, was found near Greenlaw in south-east Scotland, yet it started its life some 1400 kilometres away, high up in the remote Bulè valley below Mont Viso in the north Italian Alps. We know this thanks to a French research project that uses the non-destructive analytical technique of spectroradiometry to pinpoint the source of specific rocks.

The axehead is made of jadeitite, a rare stone of a beautiful green colour that was greatly prized during the Neolithic period. Jadeitite is extremely tough and experimental work has shown that it would have taken over one thousand hours to make this axehead, by flaking, hammering and laborious grinding and polishing. The fact that it comes from a mountain gives a clue to its significance: people associated mountains with super-natural beings and forces, so axeheads made from mountain stone were probably thought to possess divine power. Its luminous green colour and ability to catch and filter sunlight were part of its special appeal.

While this axehead was capable of being used to fell trees and cut wood, it shows no sign of use. Instead it probably served a ceremonial function as a sacred, high-status object. It was centuries old when it arrived in Scotland, brought by pioneering farming groups from northern France around 3800 BC for whom this would be a precious heirloom. Its owners probably believed that it could protect them during the perilous sea journey.

After these Alpine axeheads arrived in Britain, they were returned to the world of the gods. Some were 'killed' by breaking and/or burning them, and several were deposited in watery environments. Their sacred powers had helped the settlers travel safely – and now they could rest.

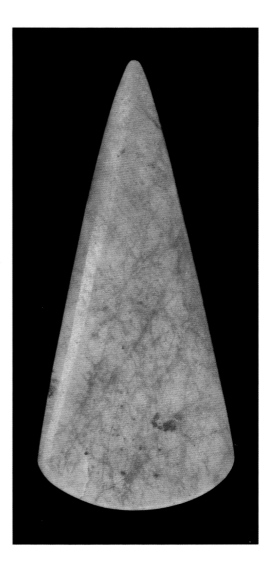

Solar power

This ostentatious neck ornament, around 4200 years old, was made from a single piece of gold, hammered into a thin crescent-shaped sheet with expanded terminals. While it is called a lunula because it resembles a crescent moon, it would actually have been a symbol of the sun, catching the sun's rays and associating its high-status wearer with its power.

This example was found by a farmer while out ploughing at Auchentaggart in south-west Scotland in the winter of 1872–73. It had been folded together and rolled up, almost like a ball, in antiquity – possibly as a way of removing this precious symbol of power from the world of the living, when it was given to the world of the gods.

It had also been damaged and repaired during the Bronze Age: the end of one of the terminals had come off, and a line of nine holes were drilled to attach a replacement piece, although that piece is not present. Whether it was just missed by the farmer is not known. The finder also damaged one of the 'horns' of the crescent, and this was repaired during the 19th century.

The lunula had been decorated with punched and incised lines, and at one point the maker had made an error in setting out the design, which was then fixed.

Recent work has revealed that the gold used to make lunulae may well have come from Cornwall or Devon. This is surprising, as the vast majority of lunulae have been found in Ireland and it had been assumed that they were made from Irish gold. It now appears likely that gold was exported from south-west England to south-west Ireland along with tin – found in the same rivers – from around 2200 BC, to be made up into lunulae there.

Most of the few lunulae found outside Ireland are not quite as expertly made as those found within, and this is true of the Auchentaggart example. Either it was made in Ireland for export, or else it was made in Scotland. This was probably using an ingot of south-west English tin that had come to Scotland as a raw material through the strong links that existed between Scotland and Ireland during the Early Bronze Age.

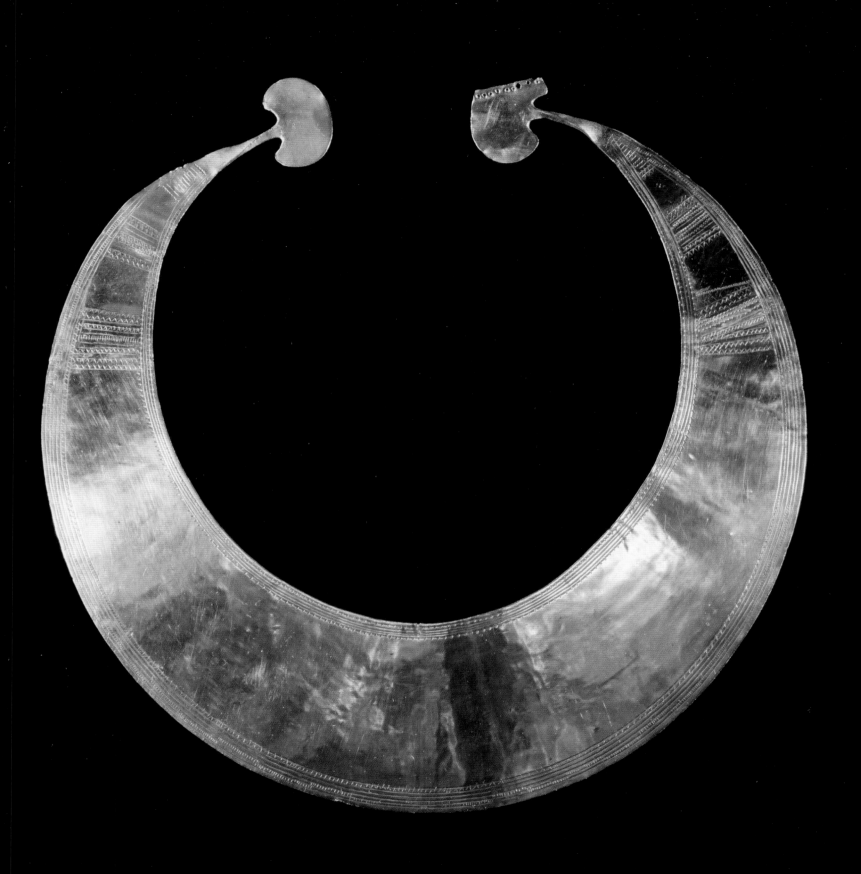

Set in stone

This Neolithic carved stone ball from Towie, Aberdeenshire, north-east Scotland, is the finest example of this peculiarly Scottish artefact type. Over 400 such balls are known, most found in and around Aberdeenshire. This one was discovered when a drain was being dug on the slopes of Glaschul Hill, Towie, in or before 1860.

It is made from a cobble of black, fine-grained stone, probably serpentinised picrite. About the size of a tennis ball, it weighs 531 grams. The surface had been carved to produce four raised circular knobs, of which three are intricately decorated and the fourth is blank. Two of the spaces between the knobs have also been decorated. The quality of the work is outstanding.

The function of carved stone balls has been much debated. They were being made from around 3100 BC. Along with maceheads and other stone objects they formed part of a range of artefacts that could have served not only as weapons but also as symbols of power – that is, weapons of social exclusion.

There is a strong connection between carved stone balls and the major passage tombs of the Boyne Valley in eastern Ireland, at Knowth, Dowth and Newgrange. The design on the Towie ball resembles the spirals pecked into the kerb stones and uprights at Newgrange; while beads, shaped as miniature versions of Scottish stone balls, have been discovered at Knowth. Irish-style 'passage tomb art' and carved stone balls have also been found in Orkney, and the Maes Howe passage tomb there was based on the great Boyne Valley monuments.

Given this Irish connection, it is highly likely that the Towie ball designs had sacred symbolic meaning. The spirals may evoke the path travelled by the sun over the course of a year. The sun was a central part of the Neolithic belief system: the passage tombs at Newgrange and at Maes Howe were built so that its rays would travel into the chamber on midwinter solstice each year.

Why so many carved stone balls were made in Aberdeenshire is unknown, but the inhabitants there were clearly connected with the Orkney élite, and they may also have undertaken the long journey to the Boyne Valley. This was a sophisticated, non-egalitarian society whose leaders were well-travelled, a major way to consolidate their status.

The Towie ball is a *tour de force* of the Neolithic stone carver, and it never ceases to capture the imagination of visitors to the Museum.

Glimpses of the sacred

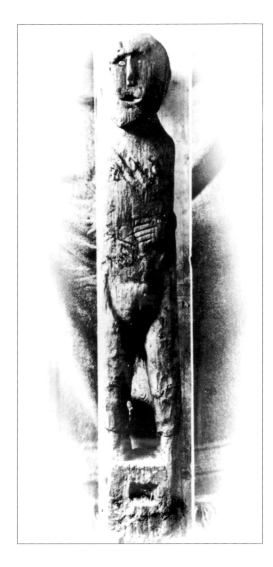

What usually survives after thousands of years in the ground are stone, metal and pottery. Organic matter is largely lost, yet wood, leather and bone were dominant in people's lives. This is why the Ballachulish figure is so exciting.

The piece of oak stands about 1.5 metres tall and dates to between 750 and 500 BC. It is carved into the shape of a naked woman, most likely a young girl. Her eyes would have been inlaid with quartz pebbles – two white staring eyes, in contrast to the dark colour of the wood. The figure gives glimpses into early Iron Age life and beliefs.

The particular problem with the Ballachulish figure is the history between its discovery and today. She was found in 1880 when people were clearing peat from Ballachulish moss, a peat bog situated where Loch Leven runs into Loch Linnhe in western Scotland. She came into the Museum's collections a year later. Conservation knowledge was limited then; photographs were taken (see left), but as Museum staff tried to preserve and gradually dry her out, she cracked like Edvard Munch's twisted 'Scream'. The photographs sadly lack detail and what she is holding in her hands or carrying over her shoulder is unclear.

In Britain, depictions of human figures in prehistory are rare and probably represent significant individuals or deities. So who was the Ballachulish figure? A goddess? A representation of a real or mythical ancestor? A commemoration of a significant woman?

Where she was found is itself significant – at an important crossing-point, on a boundary between water and land. Wet areas like peat bogs are places where people in prehistory made offerings to the gods. The figure had been placed face down, and remains of a wicker structure, perhaps a shrine, were found over the top. Around were wooden platters and containers of bog butter, a dairy-like product.

Imagine her as she may have been – a near life-size wooden figure standing in a screen or shelter, watching travellers coming up the seaway of Loch Leven, a great coastal highway, testament to beliefs that we can no longer understand.

Spectacular find

In 2009 David Booth was on his first outing with a metal detector. After some research, he went to Blair Drummond, near Stirling, walked seven steps from his car and the machine started to beep. Booth had found the most spectacular gold hoard discovered in Scotland for 150 years.

David took particular care with the find, contacting the Treasure Trove Unit, who alerted archaeologists at the Museum. Within hours, Museum staff reached the find-spot. This was Iron Age gold, but not like any seen in Scotland before.

Of the four neck-rings, or torcs, two were made from a simple ribbon of gold, with a wonderful double helical spiral – a local tradition of Scotland and Ireland.

The third was in two fragments making up half a hinged collar. Each half had been hammered from a single sheet of gold into a complicated ribbed shape. Beaten up from underneath, and then shaped over an organic core, the design detail was finally punched on the front. The style is not local, but is known in southern and western France. However, whereas French torcs are made of high-purity gold, this torc is made from an alloy of gold and silver, typical of Scottish and Irish sources. This suggests it is in French style, but made locally by someone who knew about French torcs.

The fourth torc looked strange, but familiar. The rope-like hoop with two ring terminals is a typical British Iron Age style; but the terminals were odd, with gold discs set into them, wire soldered onto the discs, and little gold balls soldered onto the wire. A chain held the rather floppy torc closed. Such filigree, granulation and chain-making technologies are alien to the Iron Age in Britain, but typical of the Mediterranean.

This story is not just about the objects; the find-spot is also important. Excavations revealed that the hoard was buried inside a timber building. The location – a low-lying flood-prone gravel terrace between a river and peat bog – was certainly not a place to settle. Watery places were often revered. Was this a shrine or temple? Were the golden objects deliberately buried as some kind of offering? Our investigations continue.

A brooch of many parts

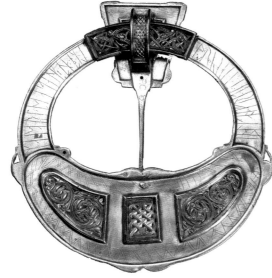

The Hunterston brooch is celebrated as one of the finest 'Celtic' brooches, but it is much more than that – such labels simplify a highly complex history. Features of this brooch embrace both the beginning and end of the Early Medieval period, and reflect what was happening in Britain, both in the 7th century and three centuries later.

Since the Roman period, people had worn brooches to gather and hold clothing together. The penannular brooch had a gap in the circular ring for the pin to move through, so that it could lock in place. Over time the terminal end-pieces of the brooch-ring increased in size, creating more opportunity for lavish decoration.

The infilled, completely circular form of the Hunterston brooch was itself an innovation of the 7th century – a new form more popular in Ireland. The discovery of the brooch on the west coast of Scotland, at Hunterston in Ayrshire, points to this Irish Sea context.

The body of the Hunterston brooch is a large silver casting, best seen from the back (pictured below). In the 7th century different types of decorative techniques, much more common in contemporary Anglo-Saxon metalwork, began to be applied to brooches made in the north and west of Britain and Ireland: colourful insets of glass and especially amber that would have been traded across the North Sea; gilding and filigree made from gold wire and granules. Animal interlace decoration was popular across northern Europe, but on this brooch it also indicates increasing connections with Anglo-Saxon neighbours, who had established kingdoms in the south and east of Britain. Many influences came together to create this very fine brooch, which is larger and more accomplished than any other of its date.

The Hunterston brooch would have been treasured by generations – handed on, inherited, gifted. On the reverse, a much later owner has inscribed his name in runes, a script that came over from Scandinavia with Viking settlement. The owner's name is Gaelic – Maelbrigte, 'the servant of Bridget', an Irish Christian saint. It was added to a complex, treasured object already 300 years old by the time of the inscription.

Buried treasure

Traprain Law is a hillfort near Haddington, East Lothian, Scotland. For four centuries it was a power centre with a two-way relationship with Rome. It is one of the most important archaeological sites in Scotland, as well as a place of European significance.

When the Romans arrived in Scotland around AD 79, they conquered some tribes but built connections to others, creating friendly 'client kingdoms' with privileged access to Roman supplies. From the evidence of excavations, the people of Traprain Law played this political game well and became friends of Rome – there are no Roman forts nearby, and the site is rich in Roman finds.

A rare and spectacular hoard of Roman silver buried around AD 425 was uncovered in May 1919, the largest cache from beyond the edge of the Roman Empire. There are about 22 kilograms of 'hack-silver' – not pristine pieces, but fragments from around 150 vessels that have been battered, cut, chopped and crushed. Was this plunder from the dying days of the Empire, with barbarians looting the province and hacking classical art to bits? New research

implies otherwise. Studies now suggest that hack-silver was a diplomatic gift, or a pay-off to friends of Rome, perhaps a weight of silver given to a warlord for services rendered. In fact, much of the hoard is cut to Roman weight standards.

The silver was found in a pit, in a yard outside a house. These fragments were probably intended to be melted down in order to be turned into prestige goods, so their history was truncated by being buried. Perhaps they were put in the ground as an offering, or placed there for safe-keeping. Either way, the hoard was never recovered in its day.

In the 1920s the Museum did not have conservators who could work on the hoard and the Edinburgh-based jewellers Brook & Son did the restoration work. They used interventionist techniques not countenanced today, which is why the pieces look so shiny. The Traprain hoard became famous and Brook gained a licence to make replicas. These give us some idea of how such pieces looked when they graced the dining tables of the Roman élite, before being cut up and dispatched beyond the wild frontier.

A Roman lioness

After a bad winter in 1997, the weight of water coming down the River Almond at Cramond, north-west Edinburgh, caused scouring and erosion. There was a passenger ferry across the river between Cramond village and the Dalmeny Estate. The ferryman, berthing his boat on the Cramond side, spotted a stone emerging from the mud. At low tide, he went out with a spade to remove the obstacle.

After a few spadefuls, the man saw the stone face of a beast staring back at him. Realising it was unusual, he contacted the City Archaeologist, who then contacted the Museum.

Staff from the Museum went to Cramond to look at the stone. It was clear from the face gazing back from the silt that this was something out of the ordinary, and it became clear it was Roman in origin. This was a truly spectacular find, and one that made archaeologists think about Roman Scotland in different ways.

An almost life-size crouching lioness, 1.52 metres in length, had been carved into a block of white sandstone. Her paws were on the shoulders of her prey, a man, naked at least from the waist up, bearded, with his hands behind his back. He is a captive; the beard and nudity identify him as barbarian, a classic Roman depiction of people they were fighting against. Beside the human figure, on the base, there are two snakes.

The lioness is a tomb guardian, representing the power of death; she is guarding the grave. In the classical world the snake symbolises the soul: death will come, but the soul will survive. However, this is also a victory monument; a strong statement of the power of Rome.

The monument dates to between AD 140 and 210, when Cramond was occupied as a fort. It denotes two worlds coming together – the world of classical Rome and the world of the frontier. It speaks of soldiers who retained elements of earlier Iron Age beliefs such as the idea of a man-eating monster.

Symbols in stone

The Hilton of Cadboll cross-slab, first erected in the 8th century, is one of the finest Early Christian stone monuments in Europe. The primary symbol of Christianity is the cross, but the large decorated cross on this particular cross-slab had been chipped off the other side sometime before 1676 when it was redressed as a burial monument for the Duff family. Only one side survives intact, but this carries an innovative range of decoration, delivering a variety of Christian messages.

Christian art produces the earliest depictions of people by artists living in Scotland, but the naturalistic hunting scene of the central panel here also has deep religious meaning, referring to Psalm 42.1, '… as the deer pants for flowing streams so my soul pants for thee, O Lord'. When the hunters call the dogs off, the deer's first instinct is to find water to drink. The figure riding side-saddle has usually been described as a Pictish princess, but many early depictions of Christ showed him riding side-saddle, with long flowing hair and elaborate robes. Could this be referencing Christ's entry into Jerusalem?

The interlocking three-legged spirals (triskeles) on the bottom square panel are elaborate and complex compositions of 'Celtic' art. This connected the Picts with their past, but here they spring out from a broken central cross, symbolising the four rivers of Paradise.

The vine scroll running round the edge is an exotic motif, originally from the Mediterranean cult of Dionysus, the god of wine, which later gained a Christian meaning through Christ's references to the vine (John 15:1–17), and the symbolism of the Eucharistic wine.

The Christian Picts continued to use a communication system of mostly abstract symbols, which they had inscribed onto stone monuments before their 7th century AD conversion. These Pictish symbols are usually grouped in pairs, sometimes with additional mirror and comb symbols. On this cross-slab, the Pictish symbol pair are a connected double-disc in the top border, and a crescent with a v-shaped rod in the top panel. The mirror and comb symbols are in the top left of the central panel, in front of the main mounted figure. Although they have never been deciphered, the interaction between the Pictish symbols and other features of this cross-slab would have communicated important messages about the local understanding of Christianity.

Hilton of Cadboll cross-slab. Probably produced by the nearby monastery of Portmahomack, Easter Ross, in north-east Scotland, this cross-slab would have originally stood over 3 metres high (now 2.34 metres).

Yearning for silver

The Romans introduced silver to Britain; after they left in the early 5th century there were no new supplies, but people still wanted the precious metal. Over four centuries, silver became a diminishing resource, diluted with copper to make it go further.

The most popular expression of wealth was through a silver penannular brooch, a hoop with a gap for an attached pin to fix clothing in place. With the Viking Age new sources of silver arrived, coming over the North Sea through the Scandinavian trade that extended across Russia and ultimately to the Islamic world. People in Ireland, Scotland and Scandinavia wore enlarged designs of silver penannular brooches, to show off their new supply of this vitally important material.

The Museum holds a hoard of silver found at Skaill Bay, Sandwick, Orkney, in the north of Scotland, deposited around AD 950 to 970. This shows the new wealth available during the Viking Age. There were a few coins, mainly from the Middle East, various types of bracelet and brooches, complete objects and well over a hundred fragments of other pieces. Much of it was hacked, or cut up; these new influxes of silver were already being recycled, as happened in Late Roman times, and hidden in times of trouble.

The Skaill hoard includes large innovative forms of penannular brooch. This style of brooch proved so popular it was even taken back to Scandinavia. The ball terminal of the largest brooch is not common in Scotland, but seen around the Irish Sea. It is covered with styles of intricate animal interlace often seen in Scandinavia, the meshed lines knotted together with just-discernible beasts coiled up within.

The Skaill hoard, its objects and material tell us much about the Viking culture. The silver certainly speaks of the vast trading networks of the Viking Age; the decoration of the jewellery expresses Scandinavian fashions, while the form of penannular brooch looks both to the past and contemporary styles. This most significant Viking Age hoard in Scotland shows Orkney as an important crossing-point at the very top of Britain, between the Irish Sea and the North Sea, and part of a network that connected Dublin, York, the Hebrides and Shetland with Scandinavia and beyond.

House of God

There was a great traffic in bones and other relics of saints during the Early Medieval period. Relics were material embodiments of the divine, required for swearing oaths, establishing churches and bringing saintly protection in battle. They demanded suitably splendid containers called reliquaries. These devices for transporting and protecting relics became part of the fabric of Christian life – allowing people to make contact with the divine.

A small wooden box (probably yew), with a hinged and roof-like lid, the Monymusk reliquary looks like a miniature church, enhanced with decorated gilded mounts and bronze and silver plates. The silver plates are decorated with very fine interlacing animals, part of a fusion of styles and older decorative motifs that Christianity adopted. Enamelled bronze side-plates attached a carrying strap. A cross is hidden within the interlace at the centre of the roof-beam. The cross was the main symbol of Christianity, but the Church was more than just a building, symbolising both Christ and his community of worshippers. These church-shaped reliquaries were distinctive to Britain and Ireland, but were also internationally important in Christian networks, travelling as far as Italy. They may also have had other functions: carrying sacraments for Holy Communion, or sacred oil for anointing rituals, including death rites.

Made in the 8th century AD, the history of this reliquary is unknown until 1859 when it was first recorded at Monymusk House, Aberdeenshire. In 1315 the family who owned the Monymusk estate were required by the king to carry into battle the *Breccbennach* (Gaelic 'speckled, peaked one'), thought to have been a relic of St Columba. Consequently, the Monymusk reliquary has been conflated with the *Breccbennach* and implicated in the pivotal Battle of Bannockburn (1314). But the Monymusk family were not keepers of the *Breccbennach* for long and there is a five hundred year gap in the evidence. However, when the reliquary was in danger of being sold at auction in 1933 there was a national outcry and it was purchased for the national collection thanks to what is now known as the Art Fund. Regardless of later historical associations, this portable Christian object is the single most important survival from Early Medieval Scotland.

Playing for time

The Lewis chessmen enchant and beguile us. Most of the pieces are made from walrus ivory, ranging from 4–10 centimetres in height. They were said to have been found in the parish of Uig on the Isle of Lewis, on the west coast of Scotland, by Malcolm MacLeod in 1831 and brought to Edinburgh for sale the same year. Of the 93 ivory pieces found, from more than one set, the Museum has eleven: two kings, three queens, three bishops, one knight and two warders. The rest are with the British Museum and some are on display in Lews Castle on the Isle of Lewis.

There is still mystery and debate about the chess pieces. Where exactly were they found? One account mentions the sand dunes at Uig Strand, while another said they were found in an underground chamber near 'the house of the black women' in Mèalasta, also in the parish of Uig. At the latter, there is evidence for an underground chamber as well as a Medieval church.

When were they made? The type of bishop's mitre dates them to post-1150; and the absence of heraldry on any of the knights' or warriors' shields, indicates a date prior to c.1200.

Where were they made? Trondheim in Norway is commonly considered to be the place of production; a comparable ivory chess queen and a wooden king have

been found there. During this time Lewis was part of Scandinavia and Trondheim was the archbishop's seat. There would have been contact between this ecclesiastical centre and the Western Isles through visiting bishops. However, the evidence is not conclusive.

Who made them? Studies to identify the individual makers behind the chess pieces have concentrated on their faces. There are possibly five different makers, who all had a good understanding of royal, ecclesiastical and military clothing.

Why were the pieces on Lewis? It is thought that a travelling merchant was perhaps shipwrecked and had to bury his stock. Alternatively, Lewis was home to significant and powerful people who could have commissioned the chess pieces. As they travelled from place to place, they may have buried or hidden their possessions for safe-keeping, intending to return at a later date to reclaim them.

Cup of the kingdom

A mazer is a communal drinking vessel of a type popular all over Europe from the 14th century. Mazers and other shared cups were important because they were passed round: a gesture of hospitality that bound people together. The Bute mazer is particularly important because of its quality, its connections, and its clearly ceremonial and commemorative functions.

A maplewood bowl with silver rim and straps, and a silver-gilt centre, the mazer is a composite object that has long been connected with the family of Bannatyne of Kames on the Isle of Bute on the Firth of Clyde. The central element, the 'print' in the base of the bowl, is of silver gilt, decorated with a heraldic lion, a lion 'couchant', surrounded by small discs with enamelled coats of arms. The lion almost certainly represents Robert the Bruce, King of Scots (1274–1329). The coats of arms date it to the early 1320s and represent Walter Stewart, progenitor of the royal Stuarts, the Steward of Scotland and guardian of Rothesay Castle on Bute; the 'Good Sir James' Douglas, a staunch supporter of Bruce; members of what became the Hamilton family; and the families of Crawford and Stewart of Menteith. One of Robert the Bruce's greatest supporters, Walter Stewart himself may have commissioned the print.

The print was originally the lid of another cup; it was probably incorporated into a mazer in the 16th century when it came into the Bannatyne family. Analysis shows that the rim and straps are of different qualities of silver, all pointing to it being a composite piece made over two or three centuries. Several other Scottish mazers survive, dating from the 16th and early 17th centuries, but they are in the form of standing cups with a foot and stem. The maplewood bowl is more common, but in all other respects the Bute mazer is unique.

Museums can bring together objects with the documentary evidence, in order to get closer to how people lived. This is one of very few objects where we can say there is a reasonable chance that Robert the Bruce saw and possibly drank from it, in some form. Very little early silver survives, but this has done so because it was an important heir-loom associated with the Bruce and the leaders of the wars that secured the independence of the Scottish kingdom in the early 14th century.

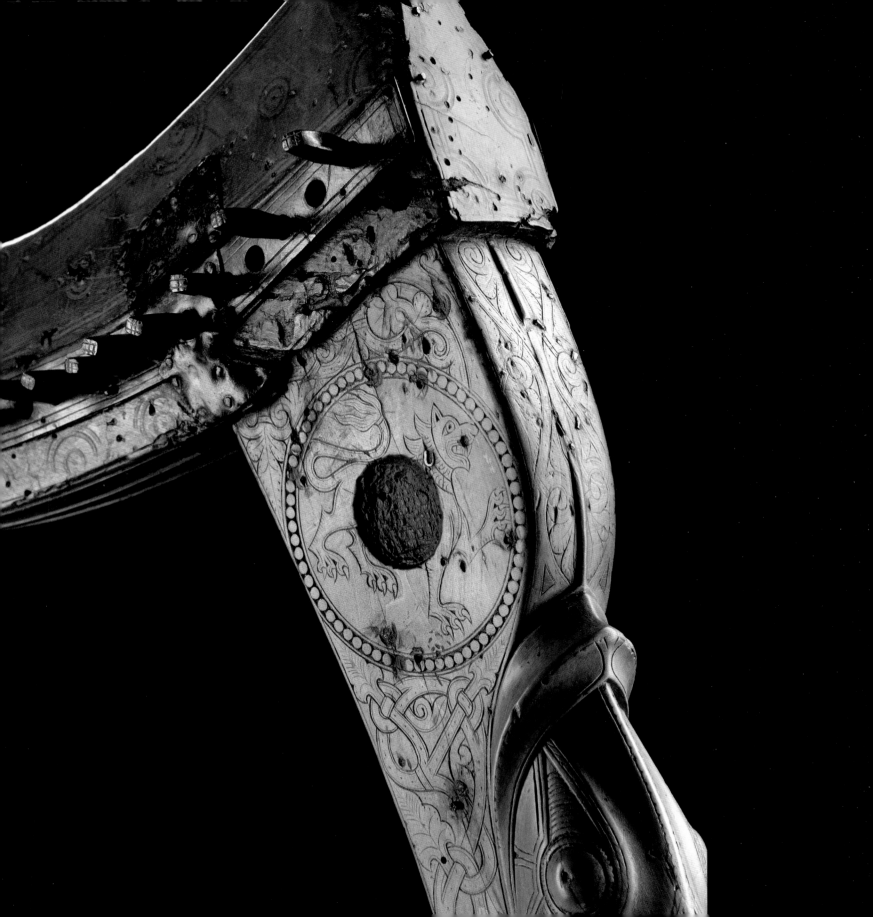

Musical mythology

Myth and legend are often as interesting as the physicality of an object. This ancient *clàrsach*, a Gaelic harp, has long been known as the 'Queen Mary harp'.

Mary, Queen of Scots (1542–87) reputedly gave the instrument to Beatrix Gardyne while on a progress in Breadalbane in north-west Perthshire. Gardyne was known to be a very fine harpist. However, in 1563, when it was supposed to have been given, Mary was not in or near Breadalbane. Moreover, Mary did not play the harp but the lute.

Legend aside, what makes this harp special is that it is one of only four of these early historical harps in existence. The Museum has two, this one and the Lamont Harp; and Trinity College Dublin has the Otway harp and, most famously, the Brian Boru Harp, the national symbol of Ireland.

So this is a very rare instrument. It is one of the earliest surviving western European harps, dating from the 15th century. Its soundbox was hollowed out from a single block of willow and was possibly made in the western seaboard of the Scottish Highlands. As an indication of the rarity of this instrument, there are only 18 or so of these wire-strung *clàrsachs* in existence, whereas there are over 500 Stradivari.

Fact and fiction have become intertwined. This harp (and also the Lamont harp) belonged to the family of Robertson of Lude in Perthshire; it is likely that it was part of reciprocal gift-giving at the time Beatrix married into the Robertson family. Perhaps to gild the gift, a half gold ryal coin of Mary's reign was put into the forepillar; the remaining circular ring of lead tacks and nails exactly fits the size of a half ryal. This was like putting a coat of arms or a shield above a doorway, marking Beatrix's betrothal.

The harp was last played in the 18th century, but remained in the family into the 19th century. The gold coin was probably taken from the Robertsons, who were a Jacobite family, in the aftermath of the 1745 Jacobite rising. The indentations suggest that the coin was lifted off by a flat-bladed Highland dirk; a British Army bayonet would have caused more damage.

Mary's jewels

Since her death, a small industry has grown up around the reputation of Mary, Queen of Scots (1542–87) manufacturing jewels, embroideries, gloves, seals and other objects said to be associated with her. Many people claimed, and sometimes still say, 'Mary, Queen of Scots slept here' or 'This is a lock of Queen Mary's hair'. Even in Presbyterian Scotland in the mid-19th century, despite the fact that she was a Catholic monarch, items were made to bolster her tragic story as Scotland's fallen queen and Elizabeth I's doomed prisoner.

In contrast to others, the Penicuik jewels are authenticated. She had them with her right to the end of her life. They comprise a necklace of gold filigree beads, and a pendant locket set of gold, enamel and seed pearls, containing portrait miniatures. They are listed in Mary's inventory after her execution at Fotheringhay Castle, Northamptonshire, England.

The Stuart monarchs always retained a great belief in their kingship and dignity of office. Such jewels would have been important to Mary. When she returned to Scotland from France in 1561, she brought back jewels with her. These were probably commissioned as part of a tradition of royal gift-giving to supporters. The necklace (pictured left) is said to have been given by Mary to Gilles Mowbray, an ancestor of the Clerk of Penicuik family. The beads would have originally held perfume and are known as paternoster beads because they usually formed a rosary. The necklace is thought to have been made up from the pair of gold bracelets Mary gave Gilles immediately before her execution.

The pendant locket with seed pearls (opposite), which contains miniatures, is a uniquely Scottish type of jewellery. The miniature here is said to be of Mary. The locket also contains a picture that may be her son Prince James, the future James VI and I, whom she last saw when he was ten months old. That possibility is part of their romantic allure.

The final cut

This beheading machine, known as 'The Maiden', was used to carry out over a hundred public executions in Edinburgh between 1564 and 1710.

It is a tremendous piece of engineering in many ways – although not as sophisticated as a French Revolutionary guillotine. It has more in common with the earlier Halifax Gibbet from Yorkshire, probably its inspiration. The Museum's machine was operated by a lever at the back, which held a rope attached to the blade via a pulley at the top. When the lever was pressed, a heavy piece of stone came down, the rope was released, the blade fell – and off came the head. Its design allowed for it to be dismantled easily and carried from place to place: it would do its grisly work and be tidied away again.

Famous people were executed on it: marquesses, dukes, the élite of the day. James Douglas, 4th Earl of Morton, for example, was executed upon it on 2 June 1581, charged with complicity in the death of Lord Henry Darnley, husband of Mary, Queen of Scots, in 1567. It was not used for 'common people', who were hanged for their crimes.

The Maiden was looked after by the Town Council of Edinburgh. It did not have a permanent home, but was transported around the city: to the Tolbooth, near St Giles' Cathedral, or down into the Grassmarket.

By the 18th century, hanging had become the capital punishment of choice, regardless of class. About 1797 the Maiden came into the collections of the Museum, although it is not known where it was before this. An English travel writer recorded that, during a visit to Edinburgh in 1776, he was shown the machine in a room below Parliament House in the city. Patched up and repaired over time, the Maiden remains fundamentally as it was, a source of grim fascination.

The Lord's Anointed

Charles I as king, with a view of Edinburgh in the background, an engraving from John Nalson's *A True copy of the journal of the High Court of Justice for the tryal of K. Charles I*, 1684.

Charles I, King of England and Scotland, was born in 1600 at Falkland Palace in Fife, east Scotland, to James VI of Scotland. In 1603 his father also became king of England. Charles ascended the throne in 1625 and in 1633 made his way back north from London, returning for his Scottish coronation.

In the coronation ceremony Charles was invested with the crown and sceptre, the Honours of Scotland created for his great-grandfather James IV. This ampulla was made for that occasion. It was the vessel that contained the oils used for anointing, a key moment in the ceremony and particularly important for the Stuart monarchy. The Stuarts believed absolutely in the Divine Right of Kings; that they were appointed by God to rule, and anointing was a material and religious statement of that right.

There was great celebration when Charles arrived in Edinburgh, with a tremendous procession into the city under a triumphal arch. Church bells were rung. Medals were struck. Yet many Scots were unhappy. The controversial Anglican coronation ceremony imposed by Charles was regarded as a propaganda exercise for his 'high' view of kingship. The coronation itself took place in the Palace of Holyroodhouse, out of public gaze.

This was the penultimate coronation to be held in Scotland. Charles I was executed in 1649, during the Civil War of 1642–51, and the monarchy abolished. His son was crowned King of Scots as Charles II by the Covenanters in 1651, but it would be ten years before his 'restoration' in England.

Despite the Stuarts' many troubles – minorities with a child on the throne, war, defeat, infighting and murder – their line stretched over three hundred years, from the grandson of Robert the Bruce in 1371 to the death of Queen Anne in 1714. They were one of Europe's longest surviving royal dynasties.

The ampulla makes an important connection with the Stuarts. It came into the Museum's collections in the 19th century. The maker may have been Edinburgh goldsmith James Denneistoun or another of the skilled goldsmiths in the city at the time. It is a small object, but it speaks of powerful forces, of belief in Divine Right – and it locates the Stuarts back in their home country of Scotland.

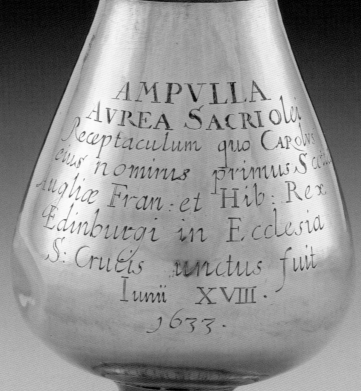

AMPVLLA
AVREA Sacri olei
Receptaculum quo Carolus
eius nominis primus Scotiæ
Angliæ Fran: et Hib: Rex
Edinburgi in Ecclesia
S: Crucis unctus fuit
Iunii XVIII.
1633.

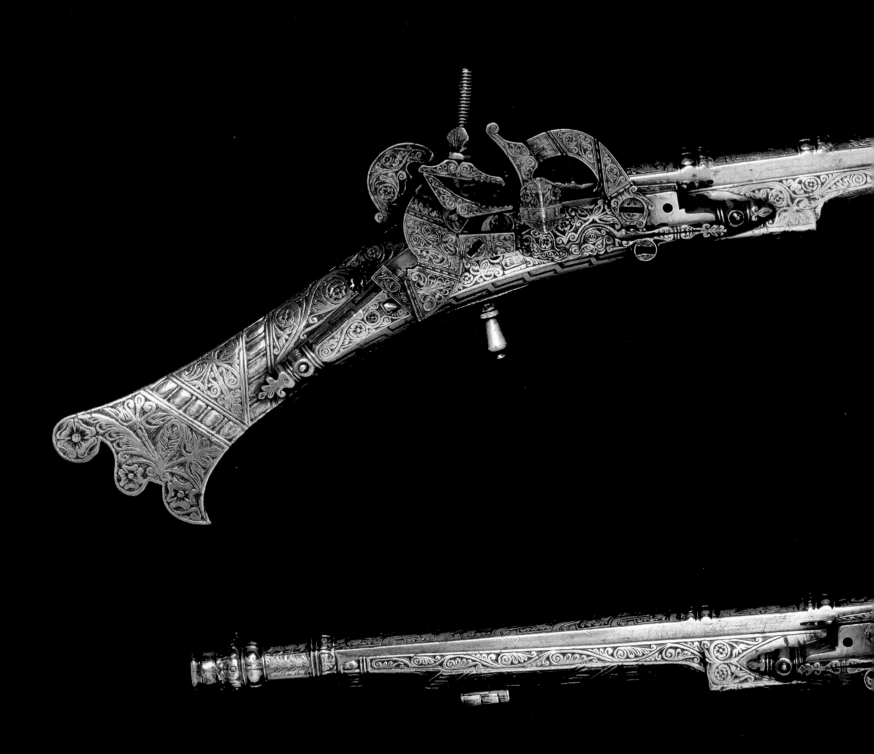

Top of the range

Pistols made by Scottish gunsmiths were sought after across Europe in the 17th and 18th centuries because they were of a particularly high quality; they were not just workaday weapons, but symbols of status and power.

Scottish pistols were usually made completely of metal; in the case of this fine pair, of brass, steel and silver. These are top of the range weapons, a matched pair made to a very high standard. They are beautifully engraved and chased, with a scroll-butt shaped rather like a fishtail, a style favoured in Scotland. Inscribed with the date 1611, they were probably made by a gunsmith called James Low, who worked mainly in Dundee in eastern Scotland in the early 17th century.

The pistols are engraved with the arms of Navarre and France, effectively the arms of King Louis XIII. The later addition of an inventory number from the French royal collection in the early 18th century gives them tight provenance. Although Scotland was not as wealthy as some of its neighbours, it was fully integrated with Europe from an early date. It is impressive to think that a local craftsman was making weapons of a quality and status that would not be deemed out of place in the French royal court.

It is not known whether Louis collected the pistols himself, or was given them. It is entirely possible that members of the Scots Guard, the élite *Garde Ecossaise*, presented the pistols to him to mark his accession to the throne in 1610. Because of the Auld Alliance, the historical connection between France and Scotland, there was a longstanding tradition of Scots soldiers serving in France. King Louis was an avid collector of weapons and firearms, and it is interesting to speculate whether the French king ever used them, for target practice or for real.

The pistols came to the Museum in the 1940s, as part of a major collection bequeathed by the weapons expert Charles Whitelaw. He had acquired them in turn from a Glasgow dealer around 1900, but before that the trail goes cold. As the dealer seems to have bought them in Russia, it is possible they came from the famed collection of the Russian empress, Catherine the Great.

'So great a loss'

The Darien chest represents the dénouement of early modern Scotland – a defining moment of the 17th century. It is simply a strong chest and a lid, with an intricate locking mechanism, of a standard north German design. Yet it held the documents and funds of the ill-fated Company of Scotland, and it held the nation's hopes.

The Scots in the second half of the 17th century were starting to look west. These were difficult times, both at home, as the 1690s were years of famine and poverty, and abroad, because English trading laws excluded Scotland from lucrative business. Scottish trade had usually been with the Baltic and the Low Countries, while England had its North American colonies and the successful trading monopoly of the East India Company. Scotland, linked with England from 1603 through the Union of the Crowns, looked south with envy, demanding a trading colony of its own.

Regrettably, the hopes and fortunes of Scotland were invested in the 1695 Darien scheme, a trading settlement on an inhospitable, malarial, mosquito-ridden swamp in Panama. The isthmus, a crossing-point between the Atlantic and Pacific Oceans, was chosen as a place where Scots could settle. The venturers might have overcome the problems of the locality, but there were other difficulties. The Spanish, who had made claims on Darien, did not want the Scots there; and King William of Orange, needing Spanish support in dealing with France, did not want to offend Spain. Facing English intransigence, Panama's difficulties as a location, with little produce to trade, and finally a long siege by the Spanish, the Darien venture failed. Very many died, and only one of 16 ships returned. The scheme haemorrhaged a quarter of Scotland's entire capital.

The chest represents both confident ambition and noble failure on the part of the Scots. The Equivalent, the debt that Scotland was obliged to repay to England in return for being rescued from financial disaster after the Darien venture failed, forced the issue of political union of the two nations in 1707.

Piping for the Laird

This is William Cumming, a young man from Glenbeg in Strathspey, wearing Highland dress and playing bagpipes – a musical instrument that may not have originated in Scotland, but which has become particularly associated with the country and its cultural identity.

This 1714 painting by Richard Waitt is an early example of what became an archetypal image of a Scotsman, the Highland piper. It is also a very early detailed representation of a Highland bagpipe, albeit one slightly different in form to the standard version of the instrument we recognise today.

William Cumming came from a family of musicians who served the Lairds of Grant for seven generations. His portrait is one of a series painted to show the family and retinue of a Highland chief and the splendour of what was in effect a court. He is expensively dressed and equipped with highland weaponry. The Laird's heraldic banner flies from the drones of the instrument. Castle Grant, seat of the family, is illustrated in the background.

The Highlands in the early 18th century were being pulled into wider society, so the Laird of Grant was a mixture of traditional clan chief and Strathspey landowner. The Grants were a Whig Highland clan, and in 1714, the year the portrait was painted, they chose to support the new king, George I of the House of Hanover, not the banished Stuarts whose supporters rose against the Hanoverian regime the following year.

We do not know exactly how bagpiping came to Scotland; bagpiping in Scotland is part of a wider European tradition of this type of wind instrument emerging from pastoral society into the musical mainstream. Bagpipes became particularly important in the Highlands in the 16th century, gradually replacing the harp or *clàrsach*, which had been the musical instrument with a special place in the social hierarchy, alongside the tradition of the Gaelic bard. This portrait has a significant place within the national collection of bagpipes and bagpiping, illustrating both the development of the instrument and the status of the piper.

Charlie's canteen

Bonnie Prince Charlie's canteen is an elaborate picnic set. Complete with two knives, two forks, two spoons, a corkscrew, nutmeg grater, salt and pepper, and a quaich – a shallow two-handled drinking vessel – it is contained in two beakers and was used for eating *al fresco*. But this set is of princely quality, and the silver and silver gilt contents are enclosed in an elaborate lidded silver case.

Before the Jacobite rising of 1745, when the Young Pretender Charles Edward Stuart, Bonnie Prince Charlie, attempted to regain the throne for the Stuarts, this canteen was made as a royal gift. It is decorated with the collar of the chivalric Order of the Thistle, and the Prince of Wales badge of three plumed feathers. Hallmarked in Edinburgh for 1740–41, it bears the maker's mark of an Edinburgh silversmith, Ebenezer Oliphant. He came from a fiercely Jacobite family, the Oliphants of Gask, who were lairds in Perthshire; they supported Charles, his father James, the Old Pretender, and his grandfather James VII and II before him. Many Jacobite supporters maintained contact with the exiled Stuart royal family, who were in Rome. It is likely that this canteen was a 21st birthday present for Prince Charles in 1741.

Similarly, the Duke of Perth gave the Prince a sword, a targe (or shield), and a complete 'set of Highland clothes'. Scottish-based Jacobites were trying to convince the exiled royal family that Scotland was the only place where there was still a chance of raising an army to fight for their cause. So this canteen had a serious political motive.

It was an ideal gift for Charles as he enjoyed outdoor pursuits such as hunting and participated in military expeditions in Italy up to the early 1740s. Although decorative, the canteen was therefore of practical use. It was appropriate that, coming to Scotland on his great military adventure, Charles would bring it with him.

It was in the Prince's possession right up to the Battle of Culloden on 16 April 1746. Ill-conceived, Culloden was a disaster for the Jacobites; Charles was forced to flee, while many hundreds of his men were left behind on the battlefield to suffer at the hands of the Duke of Cumberland's army. In his haste, Charles had to leave the baggage wagons behind. His sword, targe and the silver canteen were all lost, some to be claimed as spoils of war.

Cumberland presented the canteen to one of his officers, who was sent to London with news of the Duke's victory. It descended through generations of his family before it was acquired by the Museum in the 1980s.

Colours from Culloden

Colours are flags carried by army regiments, rallying points invested with the honour of a regiment. In the 18th century they still had a practical purpose, saying clearly to soldiers: this is where we are, this is where we form our line. The capture of a Colour in war was momentous, a symbol of victory – if a Colour was lost, it was a mark of defeat.

These two Colours survive from Culloden, a battle whose memory still carries an emotional charge. There remains a fascination with this last Jacobite battle in 1746 and its aftermath, and what it may or may not have meant for the Highlands, for Scotland and for Britain. The two Colours not only survived the battle but, uniquely, they come from either side of the conflict. One is a Saltire, the Scottish national flag, and is the Colour of the Appin Stewart Regiment, a Jacobite regiment that stood on the right of the line. The other is a Union flag, the King's Colour of Barrell's Regiment of Foot of the British Army, which stood on the left of the Hanoverian line almost facing the Appin Stewarts.

Few Colours from the defeated Jacobite army at Culloden survive. Those that were captured were not treated as normal trophies of war, but were burnt by the public executioner in Edinburgh as symbols of rebellion and treason. The Appin Stewart Colour escaped this fate thanks to Donald Livingstone, a soldier of the regiment, who reputedly tore the Colour from its staff, escaped the battlefield, hid the Colour and later returned it to the Stewarts of Ballachulish, the family who had raised the regiment. Looking at its shape, it does appear as if the Colour could have been ripped away.

Years after the battle, the Colours of Barrell's Regiment were acquired by David Stewart of Garth, a British Army officer, antiquarian and historian. His *Sketches of the Highlanders* (1822) was the first history to connect the more recent Highland traditions of soldiering back to the inheritance of ancient clan society. He was a British soldier committed to Scotland asserting its own identity within the United Kingdom, and was sympathetic to the suffering of the Jacobite past.

Stewart of Garth gave the Colours of Barrell's Regiment to the Stewarts of Ballachulish so that the Colours of the battlefield enemies of 1746 could be reunited. This was done in a spirit of reconciliation and commemoration. In this spirit, they hang side by side in the Museum.

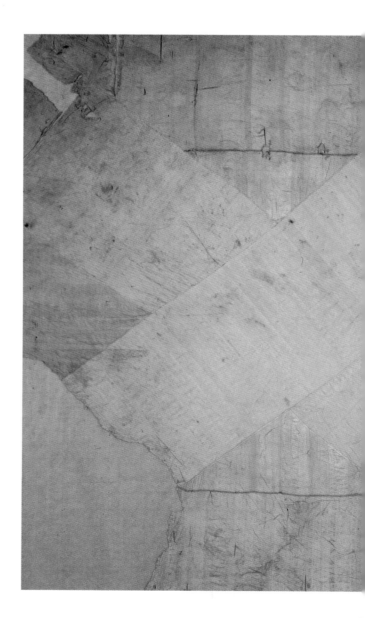

Highland suit

During the mid-18th century, tartan became closely associated with the Jacobites, the 18th-century supporters of the exiled Stuart royal family. The Young Pretender, Prince Charles Edward Stuart, known as Bonnie Prince Charlie, arrived in Scotland in the summer of 1745 to win back the throne and adopted the popular plaid for his Jacobite army. Tartan became a badge of opposition because it was highly visible, highly identifiable, and because it was a material that was readily accessible.

Sir John Hynde Cotton (1686–1752) was a baronet, an English Member of Parliament and a Jacobite Tory. He had been a constant opponent of Prime Minister Sir Robert Walpole, whose son noted that Cotton had 'wit and the faithful attendant of wit, ill nature'. Cotton became a government minister, excelling under Queen Anne (r.1702–14), and continuing to be loyal to the Stuarts even after the Hanoverian accession in 1714.

Sir John came to Edinburgh in July 1744 and it is possible that he acquired this magnificently defiant and vibrant tartan ensemble on that visit. The suit is composed of trews (trousers), a jacket and plaid (the length of cloth that he wrapped around himself). The finely woven material uses seven colours, predominantly red and green, in a tartan pattern not known today. The suit is a striking ensemble, not least because Cotton was an imposing 6 feet 4 inches tall.

Either Cotton commissioned the outfit with the specific intention of identifying himself with the Jacobite cause, or it was a gift. Tradition has it that he wore this outfit to the Palace of Holyroodhouse in Edinburgh to celebrate the Jacobite victory at Prestonpans, east of the city, in September 1745.

After Prince Charles Edward Stuart's defeat at the Battle of Culloden in 1747, the government in London banned tartan and the wearing of Highland dress. However, it continued to be used in the British Army, so by the closing years of the 18th century Highland regiments could be seen around the world wearing tartan. By the time the ban was lifted in 1782, fashionable dress was becoming influenced by military tailoring.

For the Museum to have in its collections a woven tartan that pre-dates these momentous events is unique and special.

Sounds of the glen

Although it is only one of a variety of instruments that make up the bagpiping tradition of Scotland and the wider British Isles, the Great Highland Bagpipe has predominated in Scottish piping culture since the beginning of the 19th century. As other versions of the bagpipe fell out of popular use in Scotland, it emerged as the instrument of individual and band performance, of competition, and of Scottish military music.

The Museum's collection reflects the variety of pipes that exist, from Small Pipes, through 'Pastoral' and 'Union' Pipes, bellows-blown Lowland Pipes, to high quality examples of the Great Highland Pipe such as this one. The instantly-recognisable standard version of the instrument has three drones (a bass and two tenors) that sound accompanying fixed notes to the chanter (the melody pipe played with the fingers). All four are fed with air from the tartan-covered bag, in this case in Donnachaidh (or Robertson) tartan, filled from the blow pipe.

Thomas Glen made this set of bagpipes around 1850. He was an Edinburgh musical instrument maker who started specialising in 1840, making bagpipes and publishing bagpipe music. His brother Alexander also had a bagpipe business, and both firms survived into the second half of the 20th century.

Bagpipe music has not always enjoyed the classical status and scholarly attention devoted to the history of other musical instruments. Fortunately, makers and players, and students of Gaelic culture, had the knowledge and sense of posterity to preserve some historic bagpipes. We know that two significant collectors owned this instrument before it came to the Museum.

The first was John Campbell of Islay (1821–85), a scientist, a celebrated collector interested in Highland traditions and folk crafts, a piper and an ethnologist. The Gaelic folklore he collected is recorded in his *Popular Tales of the West Highlands* (1862). The pipes were then acquired by the painter Sir Joseph Noel Paton (1821–1901), an antiquarian who amassed in his Edinburgh home an extraordinary collection of arms and armour, Medieval artefacts and Scottish antiquities.

Bagpipes have a particular place in the life of Scotland, and they represent a powerful musical inheritance from Gaelic society. Bagpiping is sometimes the butt of jokes. Yet it is much more than a preserved tradition; the bagpipe in its different forms is a musical instrument with a complex history, played by skilled musicians, and with a classical and popular repertoire of its own. That is the spirit in which the national collection was built.

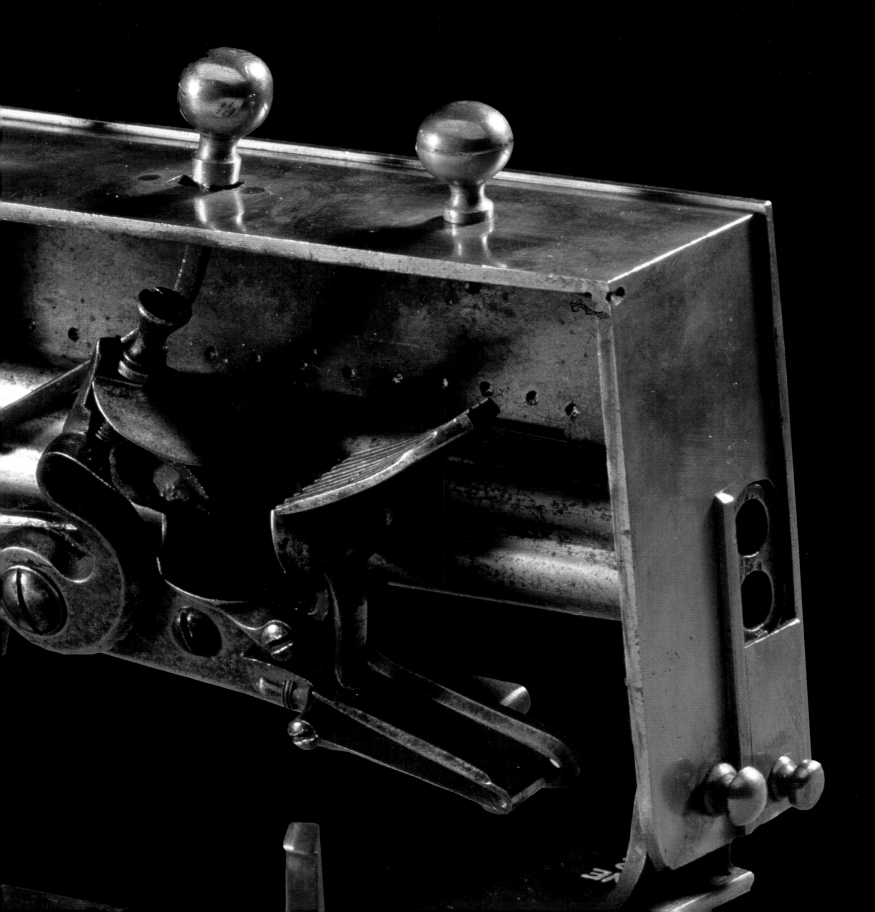

'Rob Roy's sporran'

The so-called 'Rob Roy's sporran' came into the Museum's collections in 1783. A metal cantle, or mouth of a sporran, it conceals four hidden pistols, but has no connection with the historical Rob Roy MacGregor at all.

Francis Macnab of Macnab (1734–1816), the rather dissolute chief of the Clan Macnab, gave this curious object to the Society of Antiquaries of Scotland in 1783. Sir Walter Scott was a member of this Society and, inspired by this sporran, wrote it into his hugely popular novel *Rob Roy*, published in 1818. Hence it is known as 'Rob Roy's sporran'.

Unique objects such as this are problematic to date. It is probably not much older than the date it came into the collections. Scott's description of it is fairly accurate, as well as entertaining:

> *'I advise no man to attempt opening this sporran till he has my secret,' said Rob Roy; and then … pulling one stud upwards and pressing another down, the mouth of the purse … opened. …. a small steel pistol was concealed within the purse, the trigger of which was connected to the mounting … so that the weapon would certainly be discharged and its contents lodged in the person of anyone, who, being unacquainted with the secret, should tamper with the lock …. 'This,' said he, touching the pistol, – 'this is the keeper of my privy purse.'*

Displayed in the Museum alongside a workaday leather purse that may actually have belonged to the historical Rob Roy (1671–1734), the sporran top is much loved.

Like other writers and artists associated with the Romantic view of Scotland, Sir Walter Scott has been accused of inventing a bogus idea of Scottish history. But his imagination worked on real traditions and, in this instance at least, on real objects.

'Awa wi' the Exciseman'

'*These defensive tools do more than half mankind do. They do honour to their maker. And I trust that with me they shall have the fate of a miser's gold, to be oft admired but never used.*' Those were the words Robert Burns (1759–96) wrote to the man who had made him a prized set of pistols. Why would the poor and struggling poet have needed such handsome weapons?

Burns was destined to be a tenant farmer, born into a farming family in Alloway, Ayrshire, in south-west Scotland. Due to the state of his finances he became an officer for the government Department of Excise, while he was still working at Ellisland Farm in Dumfries, also in the south-west, until his early death at the age of 37. Working for the Excise was highly dangerous and Burns received a pair of pistols in 1788 from Blair of London. These are treasures in themselves because of their link to Robert Burns, who is celebrated throughout the world for his poetry, songs, and even his love life. It is less well known that he had a living to earn, although he did have a rather ambiguous attitude to being a government employee, as his 1792 poem, 'The Deil's awa wi' the Exciseman', suggests.

It takes some detective work to determine whether these double-barrelled flintlock pistols in the Museum's collections are in fact the ones for which Burns wrote to thank Blair. Burns reputedly gave the pistols on his deathbed to his physician William Maxwell. Maxwell in turn gave them to the Roman Catholic Bishop James Gillis, who later presented them to the Museum. When in 1859 an anonymous author claimed that Burns' pistols were in his family's possession, Bishop Gillis realised that he had given the Society the wrong pistols, searched Maxwell's effects and rectified his mistake.

So were these now the right ones? They are certainly weapons of good quality. The Museum's pistols were made in Birmingham, not London. Blair did have a foundry in Birmingham, but his guns were often stamped 'London' to show their quality was acceptable to the London market. And Burns' letter of thanks to Blair was addressed to St Paul's Square, Birmingham. This all suggests that the Museum's pistols are very much the genuine article.

Seventeen coffins

Schoolboys out rabbiting in 1836 made an extraordinary discovery on the east side of Edinburgh's extinct volcano, Arthur's Seat. In a small crevice in the hill, they found a group of miniature coffins, hollowed out of solid pieces of pine with a sliver of pine for the lid, all decorated with pieces of tinned iron. In each was a little wooden figure dressed in linen and cotton clothing. Initially there were 17 coffins, although only eight survive.

From the outset they were a mystery. Were they used in witch-craft practices; or as a surrogate burial, perhaps for sailors lost at sea or those who died abroad? Investigation has solved some of the mystery; although it was initially thought they may have been buried centuries before their discovery. The coffin fixings, figures, cloth and thread all suggest a burial date of around 1830.

So what event in Edinburgh around this time would occasion the burial of 17 miniature coffins and occupants? The year 1829 saw the sensational trial of William Burke and William Hare. Although often called body-snatchers, they were murderers responsible for the deaths of 16 people. In total they sold the bodies of 17 people to Robert Knox the surgeon for dissection, the first being an old man who died of natural causes in the lodging house the pair ran.

There was a great demand for cadavers in Edinburgh, which was a world-renowned centre of medical research and teaching then as now. There were simply not enough corpses to supply the anatomy schools by normal means. People were generally repelled by the notion of their deceased being dissected because it was believed that the body had to be whole to be resurrected at the Final Judgement. Supply was therefore met illegally by gangs who dug up bodies from fresh graves. Burke and Hare did away with this process; they went straight to the source, suffocating victims in their lodging house.

Putting the evidence together, it is most plausible that the 17 coffins from Arthur's Seat represent the victims of Burke and Hare, given a surrogate burial by someone who wanted to set their spirits at rest. However, their full story will forever remain a tantalising mystery.

For Valour

A simple bronze cross engraved with the motto 'For Valour', the Victoria Cross is the highest British military decoration for gallantry. Many Scotsmen have received this honour, but few represent a more quintessentially Scottish story than this First World War award to 'the Piper of Loos'.

Piper Daniel Laidlaw (1875–1950) received the Victoria Cross for his gallantry at the Battle of Loos on the Western Front in France on 25 September 1915. That battle was the first major offensive using large numbers of volunteers on the front line, men who had joined up when the First World War broke out.

Two Scottish divisions were in the attack on the opening day of the battle. Despite initial successes, overall the offensive was a costly failure, hugely expensive in lives

lost. News coming back to Scotland of casualties on an unprecedented scale placed the country in mourning. However, in the midst of that distress, a story emerged which is almost an archetype of the Scottish military tradition: the wounded piper playing under heavy fire.

Laidlaw was an experienced soldier, in a battalion of much younger volunteers. The attack at Loos was the first time the British used poison gas against the enemy, but the gas drifted back onto the British lines. The battalion of The King's Own Scottish Borderers, to which Laidlaw belonged, wavered in going forward, faced with heavy gunfire and deadly gas. Laidlaw went up above the trench, and did as pipers have done going back to the Napoleonic Wars and before: he played to rally the men, to encourage

them to advance. Fully exposed to enemy fire, he played until he fell wounded. And the attack went forward.

It is hard to define what it is about bagpipe music that stirs resolution in times of stress. Played in the heat of battle, it has steadied and inspired generations of soldiers.

Laidlaw's award was not the only Victoria Cross won that day, and he is not the only piper to have been awarded the highest military honour. But this was the award that the home public associated especially with an ideal of Scotland. Laidlaw became a celebrity, lionised as 'the Piper of Loos', while people in Scotland remembered their dead and braced themselves for a new order of industrial-scale warfare.

Daniel Laidlaw's medals were given to the Museum

by his grandchildren on the 90th an
in a commemorative ceremony at L
pipers paying tribute on the battlef
playing the tunes that Laidlaw had
grandson.

A momentous day

The devolved Scottish Parliament was opened on 1 July 1999. When the newly-elected members took their seats in the temporary accommodation of the Assembly Hall in Edinburgh, each was given a commemorative medal. Iain Gray, a minister in the first Scottish government, presented his medal to the Museum.

A smaller version of the medal was also given to every child born in Scotland on the day of the opening of the Parliament. The Museum was gifted one of these medals in the name of the late Donald Dewar, the first-appointed First Minister of Scotland.

The medals were commissioned from the Royal Mint, with only a short time to design and produce them before the Parliament opened. Made in bronze, their design was quite traditional. The lion rampant was based on the lion shown on the Scottish version of the £1 coin. The other side has a thistle and a simple statement of the Parliament's opening date.

What was unusual about these medals was the furore they created at the time. Articles in the media questioned the award of medals to elected members who were only just beginning their work. The outcry perhaps reflected different views of the devolution settlement and rather missed the point. The medals were commemorative of the occasion, not awards for public service. When the old Scottish Parliament was dissolved in 1707, dozens of medals were made to mark its passing. It was only fitting that a medal should be created in 1999 to mark the opening of the new political era.

The media controversy around the medals overshadowed the delightful gesture of the presentation of the children's medals. The commemoration was not for politicians alone.

Material evidence of political events can be difficult to obtain. The Museum was glad to be able to represent such an important day in recent Scottish history through donations of the two medals which were specially made to record it.

Art and Design

Scotland's national collections of art, design and fashion are among the most significant in Europe. They illustrate the creations of European artists and craft workers – sculptors, goldsmiths, glassmakers, ceramists, weavers and fashion designers – from the Middle Ages to today. Their pieces are not only of stunning beauty, but often showcase the most innovative techniques of their time.

The Scottish Arts and Crafts movement is particularly well covered, for instance with pieces from Glasgow's Charles Rennie Mackintosh and Margaret Macdonald Mackintosh, and from Edinburgh's Phoebe Anna Traquair.

The collections trace their origins to the Industrial Revolution and the wish to showcase historical creations to inspire contemporary creators and industrialists. This was one of the *raisons d'être* of the Great Exhibition of 1851, and of the creation of museums such as this. The same objective still infuses the collections today.

Significant items allow us to retrace the history of European art, design and fashion since the Middle Ages; the way our ancestors, like us, sought to bring beauty into their homes and public spaces. Our ambition is to bring this to a contemporary viewer.

As a result, the collections do not only present unique individual objects, but also items that were carefully designed to be manufactured, sometimes through mass production. The collections are dynamic and evolving, with frequent additions that equally reflect rediscoveries of ancient works of art and the most contemporary designs.

Imperial ambitions

There are two exceptional elements to this sumptuous 'tazza', a shallow dish on a stemmed foot. First there is the very large sardonyx bowl, carved in the Byzantine imperial workshops in Constantinople in the 10th century. Sardonyx is a prized variety of onyx, a mineral with parallel bands of the oxide chalcedony. Then, almost a thousand years later, this bowl was married to a Spanish enamelled solid gold foot of supreme quality.

The 10th Duke of Hamilton (1767–1852) was in Russia in 1807 as British Ambassador. He acquired the bowl in the mistaken belief that it was the holy water stoup of the Emperor Charlemagne, paying the huge sum of 9000 roubles. At home in 1812 he bought, again for a considerable sum, the lower part of a colossal gold monstrance (a liturgical object for displaying consecrated communion bread), which Philip II of Spain had ordered for the royal monastery of the Escorial. It had been looted by French troops, seized by the British, and bought at a London auction by the British royal goldsmiths Rundell, Bridge and Rundell in 1811. The Duke united these two exceptional parts and made something even more extraordinary from them.

The Duke had a very high opinion of the status of the House of Hamilton. Their peerage went back to Charles I in 1643, and they had been a heartbeat away from the throne of Scotland during the minority of Mary, Queen of Scots. He bought many items with royal and imperial provenances to buttress his status, including the finest French 18th-century furniture made for Louis XVI and Marie-Antoinette.

He built Hamilton Palace in Lanarkshire, Scotland, as a great powerhouse, but it was not used to entertain on a large scale or to gather together his political cronies. The tazza was said to have been used for the baptism of the Duke's two children, but not thereafter. When the 12th Duke was in severe financial difficulties in the early 1880s, with debts in excess of £1.3 million, he sold the tazza and five other major items to the collector Alfred de Rothschild for £24,000. A huge auction of Hamilton items followed, and the once-great collection was dispersed.

Venetian triumph

During the decline of Venice in the 17th and 18th centuries, there was a short time when the city fought back against the Ottoman Empire. Led by Francesco Morosini, the Venetians captured the Morea (the Greek Peloponnese). In 1688, with the campaign brought to a successful conclusion, Morosini was elected Doge.

Three pairs of grand tables, of which this is one table, were commissioned possibly to celebrate Morosini's triumph. They may have been made for the Morosini Palace, or as a souvenir for a Northern military commander.

The top of the table is by the otherwise little-known makers Lucio de Lucci and a relation – probably a brother – Antonio, who worked together in Venice from the 1670s to the 1690s. It is a flamboyant piece of marquetry, 1.7 by 0.9 metres, with designs in various and exotic kinds of woods. Tropical hardwoods were rare in the 1680s, and some woods have been dyed different colours. There are also pewter and ivory adornments. Scenes of warfare are depicted, as well as people displaced by military operations, Oriental or Ottoman merchants standing in a colonnade with a classical city around them, and hunting scenes in the corners.

The table base is even more flamboyant. Unusually it is made from boxwood rather than gilded softwood, and has a highly complex sculptural form. It is finely wrought and animated, with tremendous S-scrolls. The base is attributed to Andrea Brustolon, a carver and sculptor who made altarpieces and funerary monuments in the Veneto in both stone and wood.

This table is incredibly rare for its size, date and origins. One of a pair, its companion was acquired by the Victoria and Albert Museum in London. Purchased by the 5th Duke of Buccleuch in 1833 for Dalkeith Palace, Midlothian, Scotland, they were sold in 1971, and again in 2011. The ivory lozenge which would have borne the arms of the original owner had been prised off and the Duke of Buccleuch's arms put in its place. As this has robbed us of details of the table's commission and ownership, it remains a magnificent puzzle.

Statement piece

One of the most expensive pieces of furniture produced in London in the 18th century, this chair is part of an exceptional suite. It is the only documented furniture made by the Chippendale workshop to designs by Robert Adam (1728–92). The set of eight chairs and four sofas adorned the grandest room in the London house of Sir Lawrence Dundas (1710–81). An extremely wealthy Scotsman, he had made a great deal of money supplying the British Army, initially during the Jacobite campaigns and thereafter with a variety of goods for European warfare.

Picture Dundas, the successful businessman, desperately trying to become a Member of Parliament, attempting to promote his family, trying to secure a peerage. Dundas was grossly maligned by London society, but judged by the standards of the 18th century he was not as grasping as supposed. Like many *nouveaux riches* he wanted to display his wealth and taste, and he did this by commissioning Robert Adam, the leading fashionable designer of the day.

Adam preferred to design a house, furnish the client with the drawings, get paid and stand back; then a local contractor would take over the building. Equally with furniture, carpets or ceilings, he would give the client the drawings, but it was the client's business to employ the workmen. Dundas had already shopped at the showroom of Thomas Chippendale (1718–79), one of the top furniture makers in mid-Georgian London, before going back to Chippendale to have these designs made.

Adam was particularly influential in developing a neo-classical style in the mid- to late 1760s, moving away from the rococo. This chair is nearly full-blooded neo-classical; all the motifs are Roman, and it has a rather heavy and august stature. Chippendale was very alive to that change of taste and worked closely to the Adam design. This unique collaboration in itself makes the chairs unusual, giving them a certain mystique, as well as – at £20 each in 1795 – a very high price.

Robert Adam, painted by George Willison (1741–97), oil on canvas, *c.*1770–75.

A rare survivor

A 'table carpet' is just that – a carpet applied to a tradition of covering tables with cloths, in a period when carpets were so expensive that standing on them was the exception rather than the rule. Instead, they were laid on tables and used as items of display. Surviving British table carpets are a rarity. This one – known as the Kinghorne carpet – dates from the first half of the 17th century. Carpet-making in Britain at this time was probably centred in Norwich, eastern England, although information on the industry is scarce.

The carpet was discovered at Glamis Castle in Angus, Scotland, and acquired by the Museum in 1985. It is believed to have been in the same family since it was made. The coronet sits above a monogram, with the combined letters MEILCK. The IL and CK point to John Lyon (IL) of the Lyon family, Comes – Earl – Kinghorne (CK). It is not known if the letters M and E refer to John Lyon's marriage in 1618 to Margaret Erskine, daughter of the Earl of Mar; or to his second wife, Elizabeth Maule, married sometime around 1640. It is assumed that this rare and expensive carpet commemorates one of these two unions.

Different elements come together in this beautiful and important piece. Its colours and decoration – motifs, cartouches, script-like shapes – have an oriental flavour, yet it has borders of delicate English garden flowers. The carpet is not symmetrical and some of the cartouches are truncated, although it is unclear why this is the case. It does not appear that the carpet was woven in strips and stitched together. Perhaps the weaver was asked to adapt the design, possibly to fit a specific item of furniture.

After much research it is thought that the carpet is likely to date to the 1620s, for it is then that the Great Hall of Glamis Castle was remodelled, with a barrel-vaulted ceiling bearing a very similar monogram in the plasterwork. If so, we can think of this sumptuous carpet working together with its surroundings to radiate the family's power and importance.

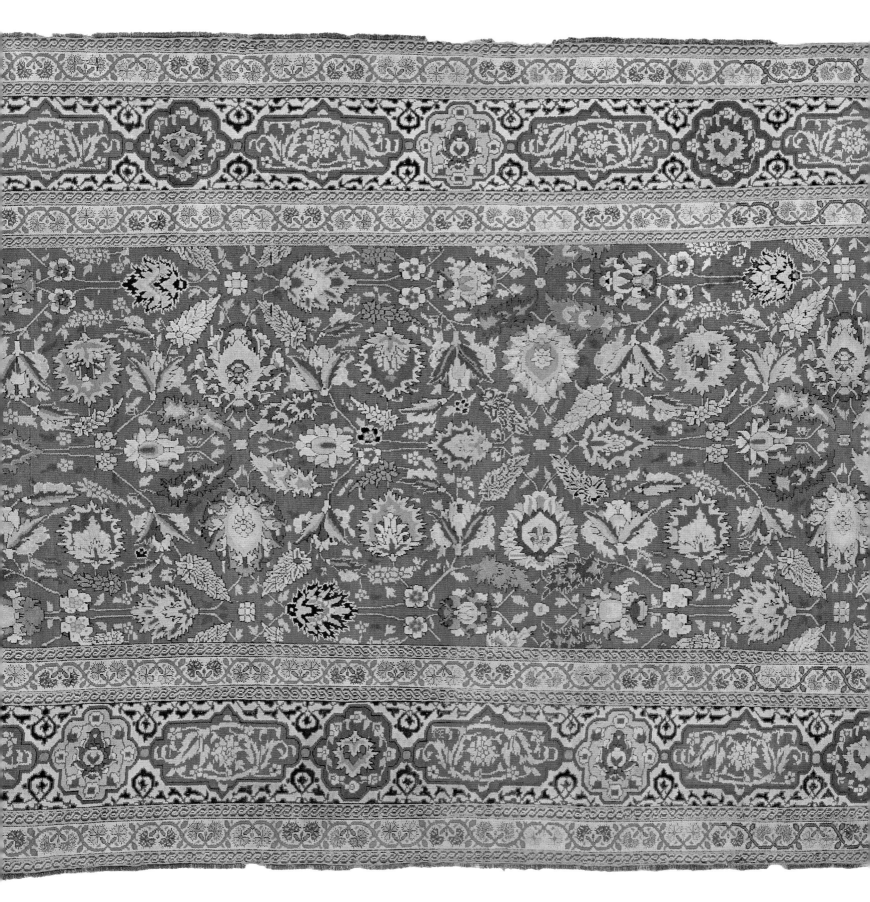

Bon voyage

Martin-Guillaume Biennais (1764–1843) specialised in making 'travelling services': compact and elegant assemblages designed for use when away from home or on active service. They met the needs of eating and drinking, and of toilette; they even had multi-purpose tools for dismantling and cleaning pistols.

There are over a hundred items in this superb service. The carefully chosen contents include small, simplified pieces and ingenious use of space. Some are stored inside other items – so the teapot, for example, contains the tea caddy. Biennais was originally a *tabletier* (a maker and seller of fine wooden items) and the chest is a beautifully designed and made object in itself. A false lid drops down and forms a writing slope. Leather wallets for stationery are attached to the back of the real lid. Under the wooden pallets, on the left-hand side, is a secret tray for gold and silver coins. On the right-hand side is another, pull-out writing surface, with a lockable drawer for letters and documents. To prevent theft, the chest can be screwed down to the floorboards of a residence, using threaded rods operated by a key.

In 1803 Napoleon's favourite sister Pauline married the Italian Prince Camillo Borghese. Biennais supplied Napoleon with this service, engraved 'BB' for Bonaparte-Borghese, which is associated with their wedding.

Napoleon was idolised by the 10th Duke of Hamilton (1767–1852), Scotland's premier peer. Although Britain was at war with France, the Duke commissioned Jacques-Louis David, Napoleon's official artist, to paint a full-length portrait of the Emperor. It arrived in Britain in 1813 and was displayed in the Duke's London townhouse. After the war ended, the Duke went to Rome and became a close friend and helper of Princess Pauline Borghese, Napoleon's mother, and also his uncle, Cardinal Fesch.

In 1825 the Princess bequeathed this travelling service to the Duke as a reminder of their friendship. The gift inspired him to employ Napoleon's former architect Charles Percier to design interiors for his home, Hamilton Palace, in Lanarkshire, Scotland, and to go on to purchase Napoleon's stupendous 1810 marriage tea service. This was also supplied by Biennais and the two parts are now held by National Museums Scotland and the Musée du Louvre in Paris.

The virtue of Prudence

The *Triumph of Prudence* tapestry, now carefully conserved and returned to display, is a survivor of an original set of seven magnificent silk and wool tapestries, the 'Triumph of the Seven Virtues'. More than 5 metres across and over 4 metres high, it was probably woven in Brussels between 1525 and 1528. It is one of the earliest surviving examples from the 'Virtues' set, which was produced several times.

Tapestries like this were commissioned as grand wall hangings for palaces and the houses of the wealthy; works of art in their own right, they provided inspiration and enjoyment for owners and visitors. A full set of seven tapestries was a conspicuous sign of wealth, as well as a portable asset that could be moved between residences. In the 16th century, tapestries were far more valuable than paintings due to the time, skill and cost of materials involved in making them.

The 'Triumph of the Seven Virtues' series illustrates the four Cardinal Virtues of Prudence, Justice, Temperance and Fortitude, and the three Theological Virtues of Faith, Hope and Charity. Sixteenth-century Virtues were the ideal characteristics that all should strive towards, but were stressed as particularly important for the ruling classes and royalty. The tapestry in the Museum's collection illustrates the allegorical figure of Prudence. Her main characteristics were to deliberate and judge by combining universal principles with knowledge of present concerns, before commanding actions.

Prudence was considered the primary virtue by medieval theologian and philosopher, Thomas Aquinas (*c*.1225–74). The *Triumph of Prudence* may therefore have come first in the 'Triumph of the Seven Virtues' set, which would have been hung to be viewed in a specific order. The tapestry presents a densely depicted scene; Prudence rides on a chariot at the centre, led by harnessed dragons, and surrounded by a crowd. The characters in the crowd represent prudent qualities through their stories, which are from Greek mythology, classical antiquity and the Old Testament of the Bible.

In preparation for display, the tapestry underwent conservation treatments at specialist centres in Brussels and Suffolk, reviving and stabilising it for the benefit of a new generation.

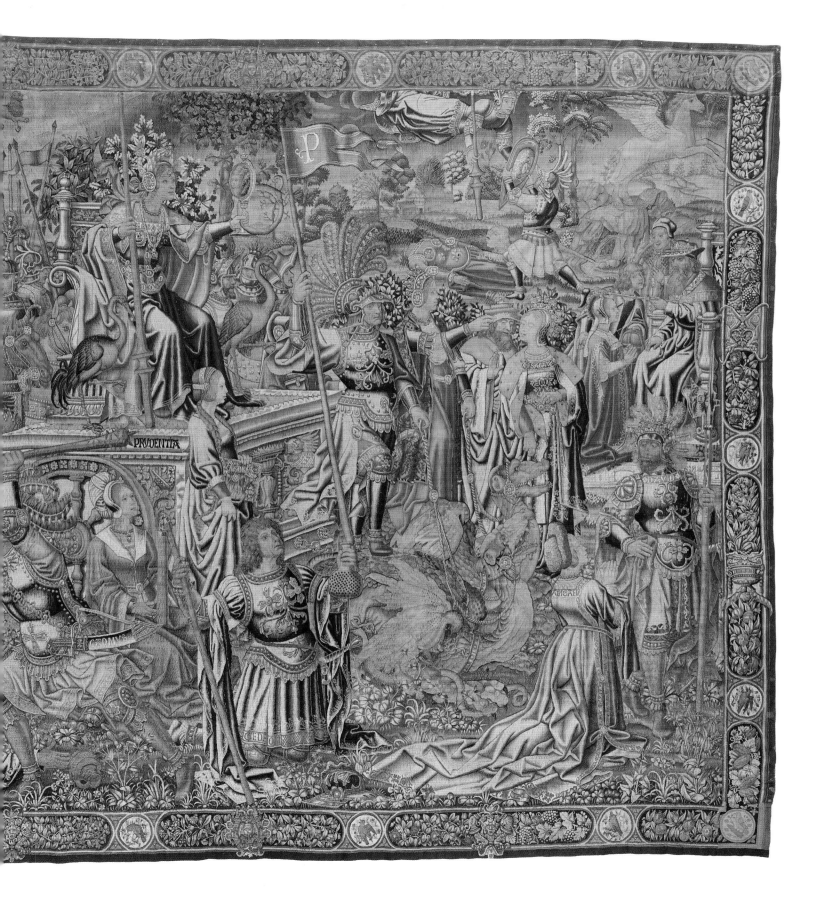

Portraits in ivory

David Le Marchand (1674–1726), the great early 18th-century ivory carver, was a Huguenot, a French Calvinist Protestant. Generally based in provincial towns, the Huguenots were very skilled at gold-smithing, working in textiles, and crafts of all kinds.

Le Marchand fled from France after King Louis XIV revoked the Edict of Nantes in 1685. The Edict, originally signed in 1598, granted civil rights to French Protestants. However, as Louis became ever more intent on ruling a fully Catholic nation, Protestants faced conversion or persecution. They left in their thousands for Germany, Britain, the Low Countries and South Africa.

An obvious destination for Le Marchand would have been London, with its sizeable Huguenot population and thriving market for work. However, there was also a Huguenot presence in Scotland and Le Marchand is known to have lived in Edinburgh between 1696 and 1700. As a foreign immigrant, he was allowed to practise his trade on condition that he also trained children from the city and elsewhere in Scotland to carve ivory.

Ivory is an interesting medium to carve. The sculptor can achieve very fine detail, and it has a wonderful lustrous effect when polished. Although a young man, Le Marchand produced fine works in ivory for some of the great Scottish families, including Sir George Mackenzie, created Viscount Tarbat in 1685 and Earl of Cromartie in 1703. The Earl possibly commissioned a small set of medallions in ivory, of himself and his family, and also this miniature bust of his second son and heir, John, later 2nd Earl of Cromartie. They represent a means of drawing attention to his own aggrandisement.

In 1690 the 1st Earl of Cromartie had established a whole county, Ross and Cromarty, where he owned a landholding of about 345 square miles. While building in the north, he also rebuilt Royston House, now Caroline Park, in north Edinburgh, and decorated it with painted ceilings by the Huguenot Nicolas Heude. At the height of his career, Cromartie served as Lord Advocate and then Secretary of State for Scotland.

Bookends

Dunglass Castle was a modest medieval tower house in Dunbartonshire, on the northern shore of the Clyde in west Scotland, before it was re-modelled in the 19th century. It had been the house of the designer and bookbinder Talwin Morris (1865–1911), who sold it to the father of Margaret Macdonald (1864–1943), the wife and co-designer of Charles Rennie Mackintosh (1868–1928). The couple moved to 120 Mains Street, Glasgow, in 1900, furnishing and fashioning it as one of their first celebrated white interiors. Certain features of their flat were replicated for Dunglass, where Margaret's brother Charles lived.

This white-painted bookcase with panelled and leaded glass doors, or rather two large bookcases flanking a narrow magazine rack, is a prime example of Mackintosh's designs that explored very white interiors. The furniture and fittings, in addition to the bookcase, included a white-painted fireplace and a corner settle with fabric covering designed by Margaret Macdonald and her sister Frances. The Dunglass Castle furniture must date from around the same time as the Glasgow flat; one of the bookcase design drawings is dated June 1900.

These white interiors survive famously in the Hill House, Helensburgh, west of Glasgow, designed in 1904; the bedrooms there are perhaps the most refined Mackintosh interiors of all. The Dunglass bookcase represents a particularly elegant and sophisticated period in Mackintosh's design work, where he had refined his own style to a point of perfection, with an all-encompassing approach to an interior. He then moved on to other types of design.

In the 1950s, when Mackintosh's reputation was at its most obscure, although not completely unrecognised, Margaret's family's descendants approached the Museum. They were leaving Dunglass and offered the Museum a number of items associated with the Mackintoshes, including Margaret's gesso panel *Summer*. The family kept the bookcase, but eventually sold it to the Museum in 1983. So many of these interiors have been destroyed and are now gone that a large and inventive work like this bookcase is precious to the national collections.

The spirit of Summer

The artistic achievement of Margaret Macdonald (1864–1933) found its most accomplished expression in the medium of gesso, which is a thick white paint made from gypsum and animal glue. In her hands it was a material that was painted, sculpted and embellished. Her most dynamic works were the large gesso panels made for the interiors that she designed with her husband Charles Rennie Mackintosh (1868–1928), whether tearooms or private residences.

Mackintosh is commonly regarded as Scotland's most famous architect, while Macdonald was traditionally depicted as his supportive spouse. However, Mackintosh said that he owed much of his success and creativity to his wife's influence, referring to her as a 'genius', and in recent years her contribution has been fully recognised. Macdonald began creating mural panels with her husband in 1900 for the Ingram Street Tearooms in Glasgow. Whereas Mackintosh went on to use gelatine moulds and fibrous plaster to make multiple copies of large scale panels for the Willow Tearooms, Macdonald began a series of ever finer gesso panels incorporating the selective use of pigment, string to form sinuous lines, and coloured glass beads.

Summer, made in 1904, is based on the watercolour *Summer* (1897) by Macdonald, one of four depicting the four seasons which were completed by Margaret and her sister Frances Macdonald (MacNair) between 1897 and 1898. The panel was most probably displayed in the drawing room at Dunglass Castle on the north shore of the River Clyde, west Scotland, alongside a now lost May Day decoration. It is an allegorical representation of the green fecundity of Summer with the woman, the winged cherubs and the exuberant plants and flowers, caught in a great swirl. The gesso is studded with beads and decorated with sgraffito, a technique unique to this example of Macdonald's gesso work. Making gesso pieces for private clients, in the form of overmantels or plaques applied to furniture designed by Charles Rennie Mackintosh, her work became ever more jewel-like. Yet although intensely detailed, her largest work, *The Seven Princesses*, for the Waerndorfer house music room in Vienna, measured almost 6 metres long.

Summer, the *Seven Princesses*, and *Oh ye, all ye that walk in Willowwood*, for the Willow Tearooms and now in Kelvingrove Art Gallery, Glasgow, are examples of Macdonald's finest work. *Summer* was possibly the last gesso panel that Margaret Macdonald made and it came to the Museum from Dunglass Castle, the home of her brother Charles.

A paean to music

A paean to music, love and beauty, the painted case of the 'Willowwood piano' is a stunning and important work by the Edinburgh-based Phoebe Anna Traquair (1852–1936). It is named after Dante Gabriel Rossetti's 'Willowwood' sonnets of 1869. The painting above the piano's keyboard is an illustration based on one of them:

I sat with Love upon a woodside well,
Leaning across the water, I and he;
Nor ever did he speak nor looked at me,
But touched his lute wherein was audible
The certain secret thing he had to tell …

The 'Willowwood' sonnets, central to Rossetti's larger House of Love cycle, are about the mysticism of lost and unobtainable love. Painted scenes from the Old Testament Song of Songs (Song of Solomon) cover the sides. The lid has ornate flowing floral designs, but underneath the lid Pan can be found playing his pipe as a nymph steals a look at him. All subject matters used by Traquair have a theme of music running through them.

This Steinway piano has a case designed by the distinguished Edinburgh architect and designer Robert Lorimer. Commissioned by Frank Tennant for his house at Lympne Castle, Kent, the piano was considered lost until it appeared for sale soon after a major exhibition of Traquair's work in 1996.

Traquair followed closely the critic Walter Pater's notion that all art should aspire to the condition of music. Her work is about reconciling the material and the spiritual: science, the Bible, Greek myth, art and poetry of the recent age, and the Pre-Raphaelite, Arts and Crafts, and Aesthetic movements – which are her influences. A true polymath in design, Traquair was one of the most important female Arts and Crafts designers in Britain. Her husband Ramsay Traquair was Keeper of Natural Science and Palaeontology at the Museum, and the two collaborated on work that spanned the arts and sciences.

Phoebe Traquair painted a considerable number of murals, and the Museum has a wide variety of her other work, including enamels, illuminated manuscripts and embroideries.

Nouveau to Deco

This 'Lago di Como' ('Lake Como') vase has been created using the cameo technique. Colourless glass is overlaid with yellow, blue and purple, and then acid-etched to create a view of Lake Como in Northern Italy. The vase is a stunning example of late Art Nouveau glassware from arguably Europe's most important makers, Gallé.

After the death of its founder Emile Gallé (1846–1904), the factory in Nancy, France, continued for 32 years, initially run by his widow Henriette, and then from 1919 by his son-in-law Paul Perdizet (1870–1938). This vase, designed by Perdizet, was made around 1920. It demonstrates the intricate and unequalled cameo work produced by Gallé, as well as a deep understanding of the use of colour in glass design.

Cameo glass making is a very old technique that goes back to the Romans. The Portland vase (AD 1–25) in the British Museum is an earlier form of this technique, in which the layered glass was hand-carved. In the late 19th and early 20th centuries, Art Nouveau glass makers such as Daum and Gallé elevated cameo glass to a much-admired art form.

Late 19th- and early 20th-century Europe was a hotbed of art and design movements. Not only were artists, designers and makers travelling to see each other's work, but the many exhibitions and publications meant that ideas were shared and adapted with great rapidity. As a result of this exciting cultural shift of art and design, various influences and styles fed into each other. The 'Lago di Como' vase stands on the cusp of the Art Nouveau and Art Deco styles, and offers an important and beautiful example of the transition between them.

Functional beauty

Christopher Dresser (1834–1902) was an important designer and art educator in Britain during the second half of the 19th century. His work is still considered influential today and he is often regarded as the first industrial designer.

Dresser came out of the mid-19th century Design Reform movement. This began in Britain in the 1830s, partly with A W N Pugin (1812–52) and his reinvigoration of medieval design, but also through government boards set up to investigate the state of British manufacture and the establishment of design schools to improve it.

Born in Glasgow to English parents, Dresser studied at the Government School of Design in London (now the Royal College of Art) from the age of 13. He trained as a botanist and a designer, an unusual combination of subjects. One of his mentors was Owen Jones (1809–74), the father of Design Reform; Dresser contributed the botanical page for Jones's great design manual, *The Grammar of Ornament* (1856).

As a designer, Dresser applied not only ideas about ornament but also scientific ideas, such as conducting experiments to ensure that teapots or kettles poured properly. He believed things could be beautiful, but they also had to be functional.

Dresser's teapots are rare survivals of his radical work at the peak of his powers. Many of his designs borrowed extensively from Japanese form and ornament. The 1862 International Exhibition in London showed Japanese art for the first time in public in Britain, and this proved revolutionary for art and design in Europe.

This Japanese-inspired electroplated tea-pot was designed around 1879, just after Dresser visited Japan in 1876–77, the first Western designer to go there. Drum-shaped with an angular spout and an ebonised rod handle, and supported on six small peg feet, it was made in Sheffield by James Dixon & Sons. This was an innovative design for 1870s Britain, taking Japanese aesthetics and reworking them with modern practices.

Dresser worked for a number of manufacturers, creating designs for the full range of home interiors, from silver plate, furniture, ceramics and textiles, to chairs and wallpapers. He believed in making things affordable and available to a wide public. Although some regard his stark and rigorous metalwork as pre-figuring modernism, he was also very concerned with using and improving ornament, and his work should be understood in its broader context as part of an impetus to improve design in 19th-century Britain.

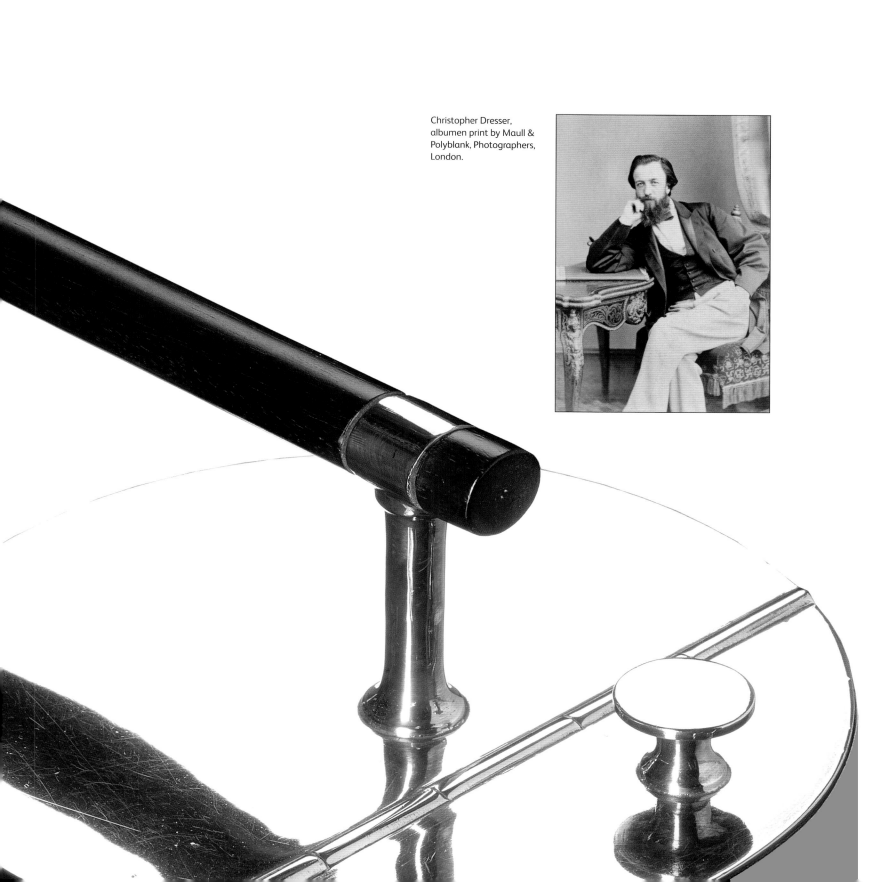

Christopher Dresser,
albumen print by Maull &
Polyblank, Photographers,
London.

Marcel Breuer in a Wassily chair, by an unknown photographer.

From Bauhaus to our house

The Bauhaus (1919–33), founded by the architect and designer Walter Gropius, was an art school in Germany at the cutting edge of art and design. The school employed and taught many of the greatest names in modernism, and was a hugely important force in the development of 20th-century design thinking. Marcel Breuer (1902–81) was to become one of the century's foremost designers and architects. A graduate of the school in its first guise, when it was established in Weimar, Germany, in 1919, the Hungarian-born Breuer made his name as a teacher and designer at the second school in Dessau, Germany, during the 1920s.

It is believed that this particular dressing table, designed by Breuer in 1925 and made of stained and painted wood and mirrored glass, is from the house of the artist Wassily Kandinsky and his second wife Nina Nikolayevna Andreevskaya. Kandinsky taught at the Bauhaus and lived in one of the 'white cube' masters' houses designed by Walter Gropius. This dressing table, with its primary colours and pared-down, deconstructed aesthetic, would have appealed to an abstract artist like Kandinsky. The dressing table with its flat planes of colour demonstrates the move away from decoration and ornament. The buildings of the Dessau Bauhaus, designed by Gropius in 1925–26, are a perfect example of the unornamented glass and concrete blocks that have influenced design during the 20th and 21st centuries.

With the rise of Nazism in Germany in the 1930s, modernist art movements were condemned by the new regime as 'degenerate'. This situation was further complicated by the Jewish origins of many of the school's designers. The Bauhaus finally closed in 1933, with many of the designers fleeing to America, Britain and Palestine. Breuer had left in 1928, going to Britain and then to America, where he became more deeply involved in architecture than in furniture and product design. This exodus of designers meant that the principles of the Bauhaus gained international recognition and proved extraordinarily influential on later 20th-century design movements. Furniture designed by Breuer, especially his chairs with tubular steel frames, remains in production.

The present-day sense of aesthetics and design, particularly in functional domestic design, is still very much under the influence of modernism. This dressing table looks as fresh and striking today as it did 90 years ago.

Picasso's goat

Capra is a glass jug, but it is also an abstract representation of a sleeping goat. Made in iridescent glass, with applied black glass for the legs and head of the goat, it is a rare piece in the huge and varied output of the artist Pablo Picasso (1881–1973).

For his ceramic pieces, Picasso worked at the Madoura Pottery with Georges and Suzanne Ramié in Vallauris in the south of France, making original works. Picasso then licensed the potters to make editions of some of his pieces and these are more readily available. Collectors began to notice them because they were more affordable than his paintings or sculptures.

At Vallauris, Picasso met the great Italian glass sculptor Egidio Costantini (1912–2007). Costantini attracted many famous artists of the time, partly because of his work, but also because of his friendship, and then partnership, with the American heiress and art collector Peggy Guggenheim (1898–1979). Picasso and Costantini began their collaboration when Guggenheim invited Picasso to Venice.

Unlike his work at Madoura, where Picasso manipulated the clay and applied the surface decoration, at Fucina degli Angeli (Forge of the Angels) in Venice, Costantini translated Picasso's drawings into glass. The Museum's *Capra* is the artist's proof and there were only seven other pieces made from it.

Capra fits well with the other work by Picasso and fellow-artists Jean Cocteau (1889–1963) and Georges Braque (1882–1963) in the Museum's collection.

93

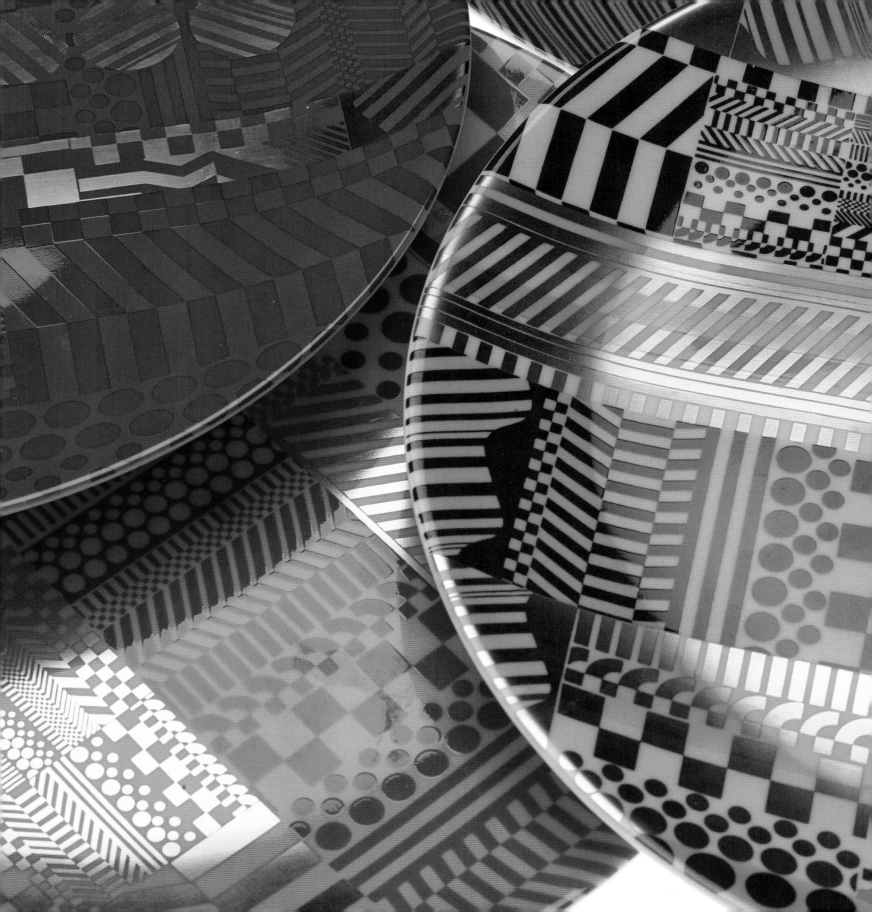

Geometric variations

Edinburgh-born Sir Eduardo Paolozzi (1924–2005) was a sculptor, collagist and printmaker who worked across a variety of media, and is regarded as a forerunner of the British Pop Art movement. He is best known for his geometric humanoid sculptures and Surrealist-inspired collages and prints. He frequently changed the media in which he worked but rarely undertook commissions for industry.

In early 1970, Paolozzi was approached by the British ceramics manufacturer Josiah Wedgwood & Sons Ltd to design a range of plates for production. Wedgwood has had a long history of collaboration with leading artists of the day to create unique limited edition pieces.

The commission took place while Paolozzi was a visiting tutor at the Royal College of Art, London. He worked with David Queensberry, then Head of Ceramics at the College, to create a series of proto-types within the college's lithographic studios. These prints were then transferred onto a set of blank plates at the Wedgwood factory in Barlaston, Staffordshire, in central England.

Paolozzi developed a series of six designs around the theme of geometry, each a variant on the other in differing colour combinations, featuring stylised squares, rectangles and circles. The resulting series, entitled 'Variations on a Geometric Theme', was put into production as a limited edition of 200, and is one of the most striking series Wedgwood has commissioned.

Eduardo Paolozzi was born and raised in Leith, Edinburgh. His parents were Italian immigrants who owned an ice-cream parlour in the area. Always wanting to be an artist, Paolozzi took evening classes at the Edinburgh College of Art before attending St Martin's School of Art and the Slade School of Art in London.

Paolozzi was an inspirational artist who combined his practice with teaching, influencing a generation at home and abroad, and is considered one of the most versatile artists in post-war Britain.

Cutting edge

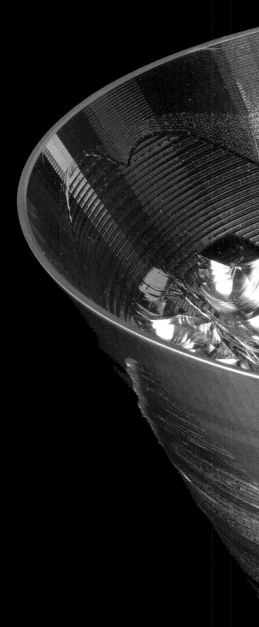

Campionissimo is a milled aluminium bowl, a creation that is brave and daring in its conception and making, and inspired by a brave and daring sportsman. The bowl, made in 2009 by the British metal designer Drummond Masterton (b.1977), marks the 60th anniversary of Italian cyclist Fausto Coppi (1919–60) winning both the Giro d'Italia and the Tour de France in the same year. Coppi was the first rider to achieve that feat, and repeated the double win in 1952. As a result of his great cycling achievements, Coppi was called 'Il Campionissimo', champion of champions.

In 2004, Drummond Masterton discovered for himself the scale of Coppi's achievement. He cycled the famous stage in the Giro d'Italia from Cueno to Pinerolo, over the climbs of the Maddalena, Vars, Izoard, Montgenevre and Sestriere, where Coppi gained over eleven minutes on his closest rival. By this time, Masterson was making a name for himself in new ways of working with metals. A graduate of Robert Gordon University, Aberdeen, when studying goldsmithing at the Royal College of Art in London he began using highly technical machine processes in his work, computer-aided design (CAD) and computer numerical control (CNC) of milling machines. Milling is a process similar to both drilling and cutting, and can achieve many of the operations using those methods.

Campionissimo is decorated with the profile of Coppi's route. The end result is a beautiful and fascinating piece of work, with intricate cutting and texturing evoking the Alps. The milling was a huge technical challenge owing to the risk of distortion, misalignment and over-cutting. The seminal importance of the bowl lies in the way the technological process, which was so successful in creating this aluminium bowl, could be applied to silver in the future.

Texture and form

Austrian-born Lucie Rie (1902–95) was one of the most influential studio potters of her generation. She trained under Michael Powolny, who was part of the Weiner Werstätte, the great Viennese workshop of the time, and was an accomplished ceramicist by the time she came to Britain, having won medals at international exhibitions.

Rie arrived in Britain in 1938, just before the Second World War. Unknown in this country, she made ceramic buttons and small pieces of jewellery to earn enough money to live. In 1946, as she became more established, she employed the potter Hans Coper (1920–81) as an assistant: he was a German-born immigrant who had arrived in 1939. They worked alongside each other for twelve years: Coper's work is more sculptural when compared to Rie's delicate pottery.

Lucie Rie used traditional ceramic techniques, but she spent a long time refining both the shapes and the surfaces of her work. Her thinly thrown vessels are closer to Scandinavian designs than other British ceramics of the time. Unlike studio potter Bernard Leach and his followers, whose work was influenced by an Asian aesthetic, Lucie Rie's bowls, vases and other traditional shapes became famous for being very architectural and modernist in form.

Lucie Rie's work is instantly recognisable: its surface decoration and the form of her pots make it distinctive. This vase in the Museum's collections illustrates Rie's refinement of traditional shapes and surface decoration.

The work of Lucie Rie is well represented in British and international collections. She had a studio in London for about 50 years and became a Dame in 1991. The Museum has two of Rie's stoneware vases, acquired in the early 1970s, and a porcelain bowl that was purchased in the 1980s.

The alchemist

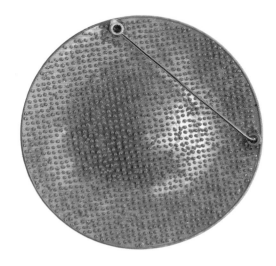

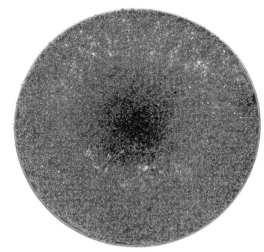

Born in Padua, Italy, in 1971, Giovanni Corvaja studied gold-smithing at the city's Istituto Statale d'Arte Pietro Selvatico under the master goldsmith Francesco Pavan. In 1990 Corvaja went to the Royal College of Art in London, then returned to Padua in 1992 after obtaining a masters degree. In 2001 he moved to Todi, in central Italy, where he continues to work as a goldsmith and runs a private workshop and training centre.

Recognised as one of the most talented goldsmiths in the world, Corvaja was, as a child, inspired by looking at fibres and sponges through a microscope. He uses a variety of techniques, including three-dimensional knitting, micro-welding and granulation, to form wisps of gold wire into sculptural jewellery. He is one of a small number of jewellers to work exclusively in precious metal.

In the 1990s Giovanni Corvaja developed a system that enabled him to draw gold to the dimension of one-fifth of a human hair, opening up a new world of possibilities. Through the intense making process, the gold is transformed into a fine thread, altering the qualities of the material. The gold then becomes softer and smooth to the touch, with a feeling similar to fur.

The 'Golden Fleece' project, which involved almost ten years of detailed research and two years in the studio, culminated in four unique pieces of jewellery. Corvaja said that the 'Golden Fleece' collection took the same amount of time to make as the Greek mythological hero Jason took to find the Golden Fleece.

The 22-carat red gold and niello brooch in the Museum's collections, measuring just 63 millimetres across, was made in 1997 and employs many of Corvaja's characteristic techniques and materials. Niello was very popular in the Renaissance – a mixture of copper, sulphur, silver and lead, fused together to make black metal used in small sections on gold or silver. Granulation, the art of applying tiny beads in gold, was also used by classical goldsmiths.

Ambiguity of nature

This tapestry was created from sketches by Graham Sutherland (1903–80), one of the great British artists of the 20th century. Sutherland worked with the Edinburgh Tapestry Company, now known as Dovecot Studios, which had already produced ten of his works in tapestry from the late 1940s.

Established in 1912 by the 4th Marquess of Bute, a Scottish peer, the Edinburgh Tapestry Company recruited its founding weavers from Merton Abbey in Surrey, the tapestry workshops of designer William Morris. Dovecot swiftly gained a reputation as one of the very finest of art tapestry weavers. The Museum is fortunate to have a number of post-1950 tapestries, mainly woven at the Dovecot Studios.

In 1976 the artist David Bathurst and master weaver Archie Brennan from Dovecot Studios planned to create a set of tapestries by leading lights of Modern British art, including Peter Blake, David Hockney and Graham Sutherland. The full plan never came to fruition, but this tapestry, entitled *Emblem on Red*, was produced – it was Sutherland's favourite work in the medium. Designed in 1977 the Museum's tapestry is the second edition, made in 1980 just before the artist's death.

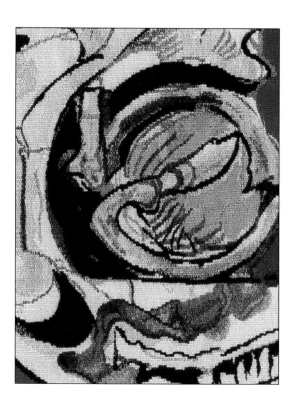

Measuring 1.70 by 1.59 metres, the red background dominates. Two stylised trees stand at the foot. A golden sun hovers over a twisted and wrought central design bristling with Sutherland's trademark swirls, thorns and prickles. These elements were, for him, emblems of the ambiguity of nature, both savage and comforting.

Sutherland's work was highly suitable for tapestry. The rich colours he frequently used – red, green and yellow – translated well and gained greater depth in wool. The sketches that he supplied for the weavers were quite small as he said he wanted to see how his work would grow when it was transferred into a different medium.

Beauty in simplicity

Jean Muir (1928–95) was renowned for making supple, fluid clothing that moved with the body. This coat-dress in the Museum's collection is made from butter-soft nappa leather, typically kid, lamb or sheep skin, which is tanned with salts of chromium or aluminium sulphate, becoming particularly soft and durable. Muir had a real virtuosity for working with leathers and suedes as though they were woven fabric, manipulating them into highly wearable, elegant garments. It was through working with matte jersey – another quintessential Muir fabric – that she learned to work with animal skin.

This classic navy dress was probably made in the early 1970s. To make a dress that appears so simple requires precise cutting, endless fittings and minute adjustments: testament to Jean Muir's skill as a dressmaker. Its design mirrors her famous belted jersey dresses, which often feature signature Muir details such as pin-tucking, top-stitching and decorative buttons. Here her signature top-stitching is achieved with little loops of leather that give the illusion it has been overstitched.

Jean Muir had a wonderful facility for carrying characteristic details of each season's designs across the collection. She would print a motif on to wool jersey for example, or cut or stamp it into suede. She often repeated these details, bringing a unity to her body of work and helping to define the Jean Muir look.

The Museum acquired the Jean Muir archive in 2005. It comprises an estimated 18,000 objects that fully document the design, making and promotion of Jean Muir's collections from 1966 to 1995. This includes paper patterns, sketches, fabric samples, jewellery and accessories, as well as around 400 finished garments, including some of her personal clothing.

Jean Muir herself invariably wore navy or black. She felt these were colours that suited her and saved her time and energy when getting dressed. By her own account, she was less interested in clothes than the craftsmanship involved in their making.

Futuristic fashion

Alexander McQueen's Autumn/Winter 2012/13 collection was designed by Sarah Burton, McQueen's successor as Creative Director following his death in 2010. The catwalk show remained true to his legacy, with dramatic styling and an otherworldly presence to the models, accessorised with mirrored plexi-glass visors and these hoof-like ankle boots, shod with a horseshoe in the platform sole. The shoes were designed specifically for the catwalk and thereafter were only made to order, so they are very exclusive.

The first question people ask when they see these boots is what does it feel like to wear them. Many designers have been experimenting with this heel-less, architectural shape, but the horseshoe inserted into the sole makes these unique. The weighty horseshoe helps to balance the shoe. Wearing high heels affects our posture and changes the way we walk, so these in particular would have dictated the model's stride on the catwalk. The shoes are imposing in appearance, but also intriguing in relation to body image.

The Autumn/Winter 2012/13 collection was inspired by nature – as McQueen's own work often was – and designed to celebrate, in Burton's words, 'a beautiful future, positivity, optimism'. The clothes in the catwalk show initially appeared as pure white, but progressed to a grand finale of theatrical looks in red and black, reflecting the journey from innocence to experience. Topped and tailed with eye-catching accessories, the show presented a dream-like spectacle.

The Museum purchased these boots from eBay, along with their original tags. Although this method of purchase is not so unusual today, these were quite a find. Fortunately, the authenticity of contemporary fashion pieces can be checked with the designers themselves and online sale opens up an exciting new avenue for building museum collections.

Surrealist couture

Elsa Schiaparelli's work during the 1930s and 1940s represents the height of her creativity, when she was famously collaborating with the Surrealist artists Jean Cocteau, Salvador Dali and Leonor Fini. This evening jacket is from her Autumn/Winter 1937/38 collection, described in *Women's Wear Daily* as a collection 'full of modern baroque whimsy'.

The delicate silk velvet carries the surface embellishment and witty detailing for which Schiaparelli is renowned, with embroidery of cast gilt metal vine leaves and glass droplets by the embroidery house Maison Lesage. Founded in 1924, Lesage took over the workshop of the established embroiderer Michonet, famous for undertaking special commissions for the court of Napoleon III and supplying the greatest names in Parisian couture, from Worth to Madeleine Vionnet. Lesage continued in its footsteps, forging special relationships with designers such as Yves Saint Laurent. More recently, in 2002, the workshop became part of Chanel's *Metiers d'art*, the artisan partners who contribute fabric buttons and decorative finishes to their collections.

This is assumed to be a favourite design of Schiaparelli's, since she chose an almost identical jacket for her famous photographic portrait by Horst P Horst for *Vogue* magazine in 1937. It differed only in the fact that Schiaparelli's was slightly longer, with long pendant front pockets, and carried the applied gold braid all the way round the back.

Curators acquired this piece at auction as it complements the Museum's collection of clothing which belonged to Frances Farquharson, formerly a fashion editor for *Vogue* and *Harper's Bazaar* in the 1920s and '30s. At this time Farquharson acquired a wardrobe of illustrious names, but Schiaparelli appears to have been a particular favourite as she had a number of her hats, evening gowns and coats among her collection.

Elsa Schiaparelli is acclaimed for her opulent detailing, Surrealist inspiration and sense of humour. The pieces the Museum has from Farquharson's collection are all beautifully cut, with some whimsical touches – a black velour coat, for example, on closer inspection turns out to have buttons with angel heads sculpted in relief. At the same time the pieces, as a whole, are quite subtle.

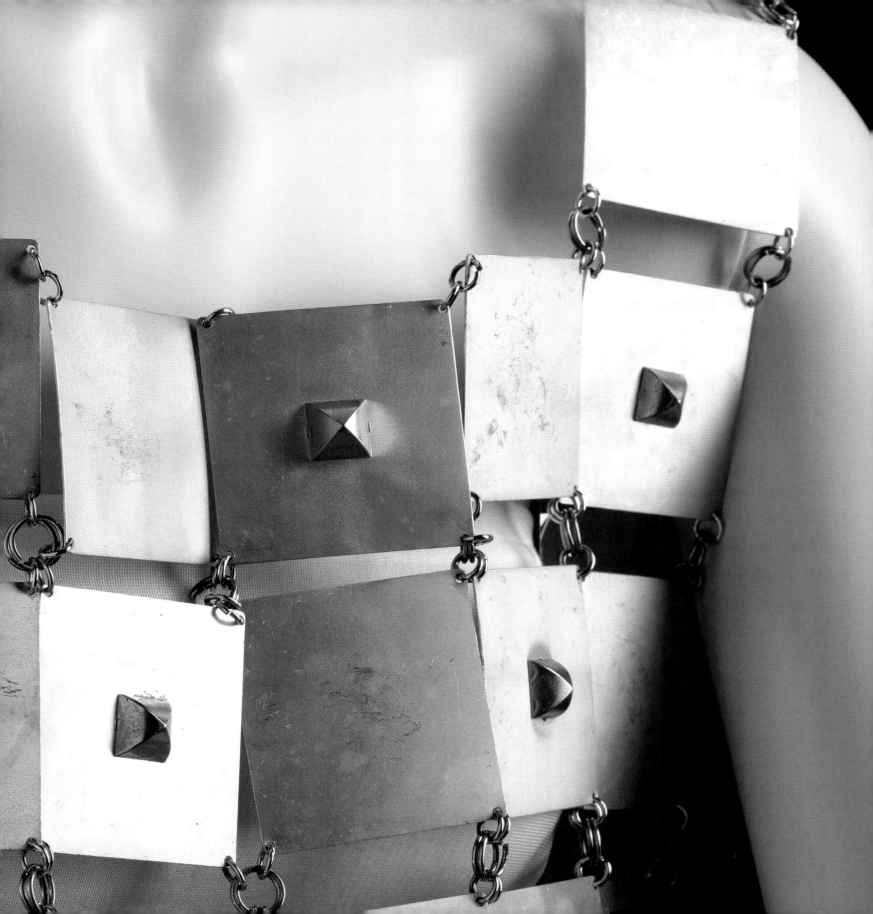

Haute couture chainmail

The 1960s conjures up images of Space Age fashions, miniskirts and go-go boots. One of the most recognisable styles of the decade was designed by Paco Rabanne (b.1934). The Spanish-born designer presented his first haute couture collection in Paris in 1966, titled '12 Unwearable Dresses in Contemporary Materials'.

Informed by his architectural background and inspired by the public interest in space travel, he surprised the world with his ingenious use of industrial materials such as metal and thread-linked plastics. He borrowed techniques from jewellery-making, creating small squares of metal which he linked together and draped over the body. As one of the first fashion designers to move beyond the idea that only fabric could be used to make garments, metal quickly became his signature material.

Despite being scandalously see-through, Rabanne's chainmail dresses became some of the most photographed of the decade and were worn by Audrey Hepburn in the film *Two for the Road* and Jane Fonda in *Barbarella*. *Vogue* published now famous images of the iconic 1960s model Donyale Luna by renowned photographers Guy Bourdin and Richard Avedon.

The design begs the question of what you might wear underneath, and therefore whether these were even worn in reality, but the Museum's tunic certainly shows signs of wear.

The tunic is a recent addition to the Museum's collections. Trends in the 1960s are often credited to a few figureheads of fashion – Mary Quant, for example, is associated with the miniskirt, while Yves Saint Laurent debuted the *Le Smoking* Tuxedo. The French designer André Courrèges introduced the revolutionary intergalactic look, while Zandra Rhodes burst onto the scene with romantic garments in arresting prints. Each of these quintessential designers is already represented in the collections – and the acquisition of the Paco Rabanne metal tunic enables the Museum to represent other pioneering designers who defined the mood of the era.

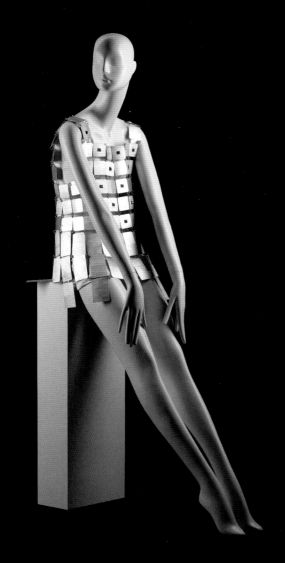

Making an entrance

By the mid-18th century this impressive mantua was a style of dress worn only at court. As it was designed to be a luxurious garment, exclusive fabrics such as this silk brocade, accentuated by gold thread and gilt lace, were an expression of the wearer's status.

The mantua was created entirely by hand, from weaving the silk and making the lace to sewing the dress together. The quality of the materials and the technical skill necessary to weave them made these fabrics very expensive – it is probable that the silk alone would cost the equivalent of around £4000 today.

It is a dress in two parts – a bodice with an attached train, and a matching petticoat. It would have been worn with a stomacher, a triangular piece of fabric inserted into the open front of the dress, as well as the finest lace accessories. A woman wore stays underneath to create the fashionable conical upper body shape, and a hooped petticoat that supported the weight of the skirts in their broad fan shape. Layers of heavy petticoats and a chemise completed the ensemble – all of which causes us to wonder what it would have been like to wear, and indeed walk, in one. Certainly, contemporary accounts demonstrate that it took skill and practice to accomplish walking and dancing in it.

The mantua was originally adopted as a new type of fashionable women's dress in late 17th-century Britain and gradually evolved in style. By the early 18th century it was the formal dress of choice. However, as the sack dress or *robe à la française* became the prevailing fashion of the day, it was reserved for court occasions. Although the extraordinarily wide skirts mirrored the general fashion, the sheer exaggeration was an affectation of court dress, and ideal for showing off the elaborately patterned silks.

We believe this mantua belonged to an ancestor of the Earl of Haddington. It dates to the time when Thomas Hamilton, 7th Earl of Haddington, held the title and estates in East Lothian, Scotland, and the dress perhaps belonged either to Mary, Countess of Haddington, or to her daughter. They reportedly led a socially active life with their peers and it is likely that this mantua would have been worn for a special occasion at the British royal court.

Natural Sciences

The origins of the Natural Sciences collections may be traced back to the acquisition in 1694 by the Toun College of Edinburgh (later the University of Edinburgh) of the collection of the late Sir Andrew Balfour. However, the vast majority of the founding collections were built up by Robert Jameson, Regius Professor of Natural History from 1804 until 1854.

The collections were developed by forebears such as the early 19th-century French ornithologist Louis Dufresne, the famous Scottish geologists Hugh Miller and Charles Peach, and include insects collected by Charles Darwin.

Since then the collections have been added to considerably and continue to be an inspiration for research and understanding of the world around us. Today our diverse Natural Sciences collections are comprehensive in their coverage of the natural world, with the exception of Botany which is represented by fossil plants. Most of the several million specimens originate from efforts to understand better the natural world through contemporary research programmes conducted by museum scientists and collaborators across Scotland and the rest of the world.

Our fossil collections are renowned globally for specimens of the now-extinct eurypterids and plants, and our fossil fish and early tetrapod collections are among the largest and most diverse in the world, providing comprehensive early records of vertebrate life. The minerals include examples from important historical Scottish mining areas, unusual igneous rocks from inaccessible regions, and a small but diverse meteorite collection. The Invertebrate Biology collection is a treasure house of diversity, ranging from sponges, jellyfish, shrimps and crabs, to worms, snails, octopuses, and sea urchins. Together they form an invaluable resource for the research of British marine fauna, especially the North Atlantic deep sea. The Vertebrate Biology collections include skins, skeletons, eggs and nests, together with tissue samples and archaeological remains. A highlight is the collection of whales, which ranks as one of the top five in the world. The Entomology collection contains material from all over the world and is a hub of research and information about Scottish insects. The insect and vertebrate collections are also significant as historical archives of terrestrial environmental change, highly relevant to pressing issues such as global warming.

A founding collection

Type specimen (above) of Giant White butterfly, *Pieris josephina*, Central America; and a selection of beetles (opposite) from the Dufresne collection.

In one sense, Louis Dufresne (1752–1832) founded this Museum. The University of Edinburgh bought his natural history collection in 1819 and used it to found the basis of the University Museum. That was in turn given to the newly-built Edinburgh Museum of Science and Art, forerunner of the Museum today, as part of its founding collection in 1866.

Dufresne was a taxidermist, curator and dealer in natural history, and also the conservator for the private collection of the French Empress Josephine (1763–1814), wife of Napoleon. The Dufresne collection was originally hers. When it was sold it was said to be the biggest in the world, and every major European institution was eager to acquire it.

Josephine had fallen out of favour with Napoleon by 1810 for failing to provide him with an heir, and she could no longer maintain the collection on her allowance. Dufresne put so much of his own money into it that eventually he owned it. In need of money himself, he then sold the collection. Against the odds, the University of Edinburgh was the successful purchaser, paying at least £2500, equivalent to millions today.

The collection comprised 3800 species in 300 genera, including almost 1000 sorts of butterfly. Many of those, including *Pieris josephina*, otherwise *Ascia* (*Ganyra*) *josephina*, the Giant White butterfly from Central America, are the invaluable 'type' specimens against which all others are compared. The great majority of the butterfly specimens have survived, which is remarkable over the course of 200 years, given their fragility. Regrettably there are few out of the 1600 bird specimens left. The collection included one of only three specimens of the Mauritius pigeon, by then extinct.

The butterfly material in the collection has three principal origins: America and the West Indies, West Africa, and Australia and the East Indies. The material from Australia was undoubtedly from the French scientific and land-scouting expedition of 1800–1803, led by Nicolas Baudin, who died on the way back. When the expedition returned, Empress Josephine specified what she wanted from the fruits of their voyage. The kangaroos, for example, were sent to live in Malmaison, Josephine's celebrated rose garden, but failed to survive. Other treasures now lie in environmentally controlled conditions in trays and cases in Edinburgh.

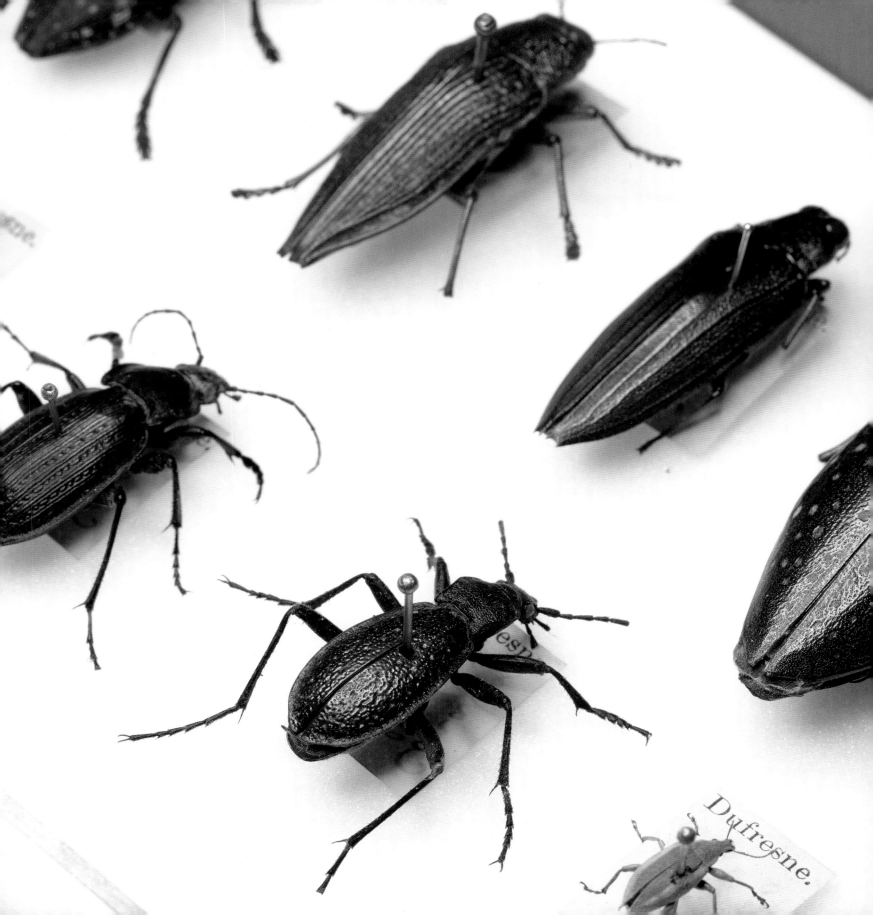

Dufresne.

Evolving interests

I will give a proof of my zeal [in collecting beetles]: *one day, on tearing off some old bark, I saw two rare beetles and seized one in each hand; then I saw a third and new kind, which I could not bear to lose, so that I popped the one which I held in my right hand into my mouth. Alas it ejected some intensely acrid fluid, which burnt my tongue so that I was forced to spit the beetle out, which was lost, as well as the third one.*

Beetle collecting was almost a national craze at the time Charles Darwin (1809–82) recalled this nasty moment in his autobiography. Although Darwin's famous beetle collections date from his Cambridge student days, his enthusiasm must have begun while attending the University of Edinburgh between 1825 and 1827.

Darwin tried and failed to complete his studies in medicine at the University of Edinburgh. He found the lectures dull, and the sight of blood repelled him. However, while in Edinburgh, he attended other lectures by the great American ornithologist, John James Audubon. And a freed Guyanan slave, a man called John Edmonstone, taught him how to stuff birds.

From 1828 Darwin studied at the University of Cambridge where he developed his interest in collecting beetles. His growing passion for natural history was then greatly influenced by botanist John Henslow and geologist Adam Sedgewick. Soon after graduating from Cambridge in 1831, Darwin was offered

the chance to be the naturalist on the second voyage of the HMS *Beagle*, a voyage that was to change his life and history.

With a single exception, the beetles that Darwin acquired, which are in the Museum's collections, were only known from Scotland. Five of the specimens are the longhorn beetle, *Pogonocherus fasciculatus*, which was unknown in England in Darwin's time. A single water beetle, *Graphoderus cinereus*, apparently came from Cambridge and was collected in 1831.

These specimens came originally from the collection of William Darwin Fox; the two are known to have exchanged many specimens. Some items, which came to the Museum in 1922, still have labels in Charles Darwin's own handwriting.

That Charles Darwin quit his medical studies in Edinburgh was fortunate for the rest of the world, and part of his legacy lies in a tray of beetle specimens in the collections of this Museum.

Charles Darwin, detail from a carte-de-visite by the London Stereoscopic & Photographic Company Limited, London.

A challenging size

This giant clamshell (*Tridacna gigas*) was brought back by John Murray from the HMS *Challenger* expedition (1872–76) as a souvenir. The two shell halves or valves weigh 143 kilograms, and with the animal inside it would have weighed considerably more. *Tridacna gigas* is usually claimed to be the world's largest bivalve; the biggest recorded example weighed an estimated 340 kilograms alive and may have lived for more than a century. In the Indo Pacific they are eaten and the shells used for practical purposes and decoration. They are classed as vulnerable by the International Union for Conservation of Nature.

Giant clams are fascinating. They cannot close their shell fully, so the brightly coloured mantle of the animal can be seen within. This colouration is caused by the algae that live inside the clam's mantle tissues and pigments made by the clam that act as a protective sun-screen. By day, the clam opens more and extends its mantle tissue for the algae to receive the sunlight required to photosynthesise. In return for a home the algae provide supplementary nutrition for the clam, which also filter-feeds. This need for sunlight limits the depth at which giant clams can live.

John Murray (1841–1914) was born in Canada, but moved to Edinburgh where he began, but did not complete, a medical degree. Instead he worked as ship's surgeon on a whaler, studied geology and scientific instrumentation and became interested in marine biology and oceanography before joining the scientific team on HMS *Challenger*. On his return, Murray was made chief assistant of the *Challenger* office in Edinburgh, and after the death of Sir Wyville Thomson, chief scientist, Murray was appointed director and published more than 50 volumes of expedition research. He started the first marine biology laboratory in the United Kingdom, at Granton, north Edinburgh, the forerunner of the Scottish Association for Marine Sciences, and was knighted in 1898.

The *Challenger* expedition is considered the foundation for modern oceanography, exploring 127,000 kilometres of ocean and returning home with numerous photographs, drawings, measurements and samples, including around 4700 previously unknown species. It was a massive achievement.

Model of HMS *Challenger*, the corvette used for the oceanographic expedition of 1872–76. Model made by H J Boyd, Edinburgh.

Gentle giant

The Japanese spider crab or takaashigani, *Macrocheira kaempferi,* has a particularly impressive leg span. If you were able to stretch out the front legs (chelipeds) of a mature male, its span could reach 3.8 metres from claw to claw.

Spider crabs belong to a group known as arthropods – invertebrate animals with external skeletons, segmented bodies and jointed legs – which also includes spiders, centipedes, insects, lobsters, shrimp and barnacles. The Japanese spider crab, weighing up to 20 kilograms, is not quite the heaviest arthropod – which is the American lobster – but it certainly has the greatest leg span of any known living member of the group. It probably became this size for protection – large octopuses being among its few predators.

The Japanese spider crab is considered a delicacy in Japan, where it lives off the coasts of the southern islands in the Pacific Ocean. It hides in crevices – holes, depressions and vents – usually at depths of 150 to 300 metres, but it is occasionally found much further down at depths of 600 metres. Females migrate upwards to around 50 metres deep during the breeding season because the juveniles cannot tolerate the colder temperatures of deeper waters.

Although the crab appears rather intimidating, these animals are reported to be quite gentle. They do not fight with each other, and their claws, which are fairly weak, are used for feeding and only to snap at creatures that try to bother them. They are quite slow-moving despite their enormous leg-size, crawling sedately across the seabed looking for dead and decaying matter to feed upon.

First described by Western science in 1836, the crab is named for the late 17th-century German explorer and naturalist, Engelbert Kaempfer. Kaempfer wrote his *History of Japan*, which was published in 1727 after his death. This became an important source of knowledge about Japan during a long period of restricted access prior to 1858.

The Museum collects marine invertebrates – sponges, sea anemones, bristleworms, shrimps, clams, starfish and more – on a large scale, and currently has over two million specimens. There is, however, only one *Macrocheira kaempferi.*

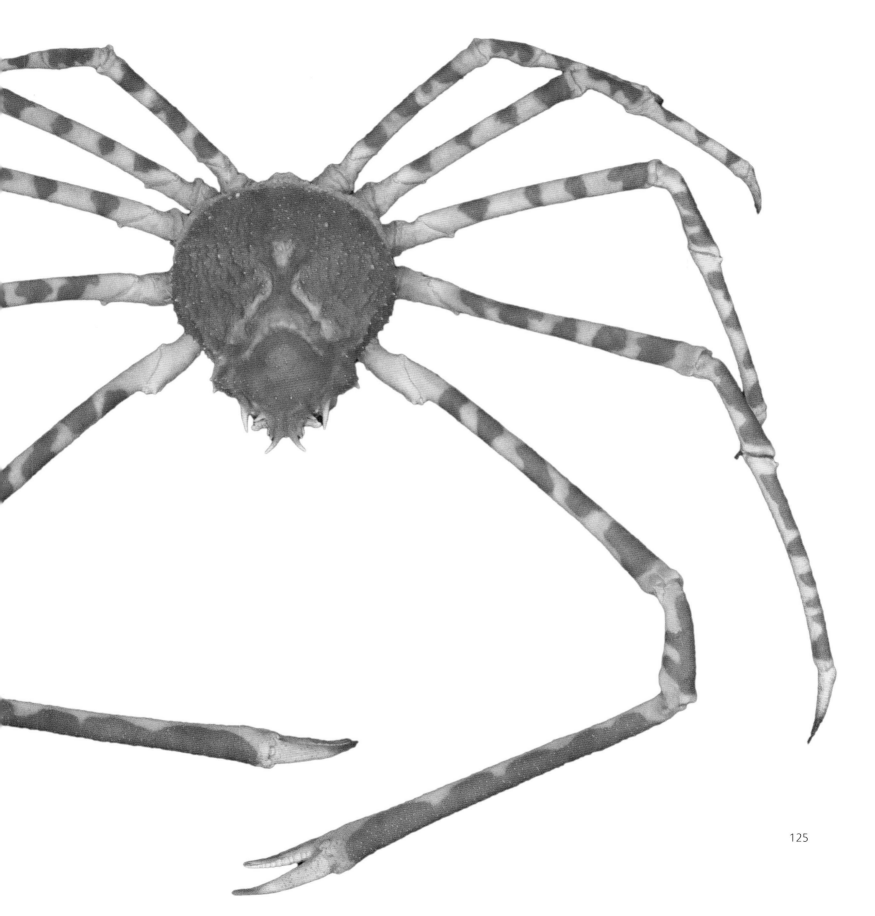

125

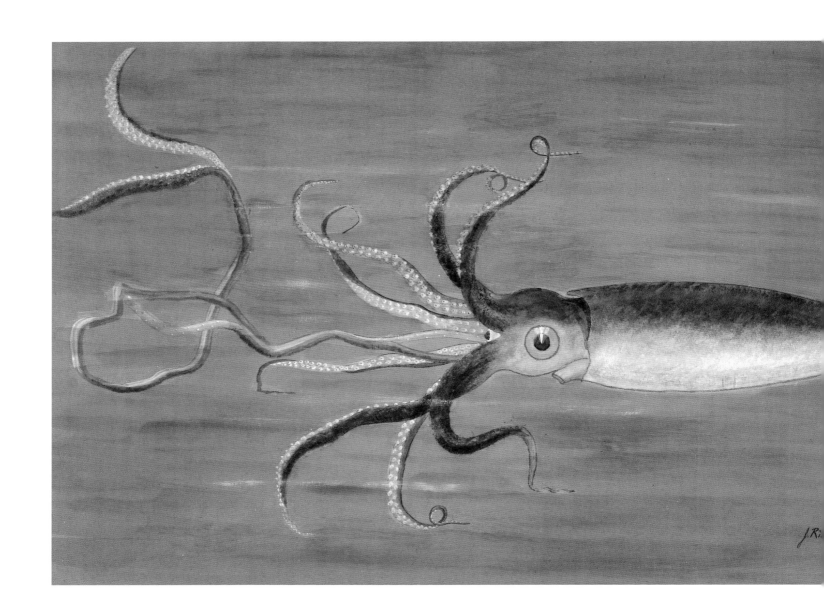

Giant of the deep

The drawing represents the Haddingtonshire giant squid (Architeuthis harveyi) as it must have appeared when alive. The colours have been noted while the specimen was fresh. Like lesser squids, this enormous example moved backwards by projecting a strong jet of water from the 'funnel' underneath its head. The two long or tentacular arms, each fourteen feet long, are represented as temporarily united by the small suckers which they use to increase their power of cohesion, and therefore their strength. The drawing is made to proportion and shows the squid on a scale of two inches to one foot or one-sixth the natural size.

This caption accompanied the original illustration (pictured) by James Ritchie, then a curator at the Museum, later to become Keeper of Natural History and President of the Royal Society of Edinburgh. In 1917 a newspaper article alerted Ritchie to a giant squid washed up in East Lothian, formerly Haddingtonshire in eastern Scotland. When he got to the beach, the squid was somewhat mutilated, presumably by earlier visitors, and almost certainly smelled terrible. He took back to the Museum a tentacle club which was subsequently preserved in a jar that stands 61.5 centimetres tall. The following year he published an article on 'the only definite occurrence of a giant squid (*Architeuthis*) on the coasts of Great Britain'.

There is still little known about Giant squid, although in the invertebrate world they are exceeded only by the Colossal squid. The first time a Giant squid was imaged while alive in its natural habitat was in 2004, and it was as recently as 2013 that scientists showed by genetic analysis that there is only one species, *Architeuthis dux*. They are generally found below 300 metres, so the comparatively shallow North Sea is probably not a suitable habitat. It is not known how this specimen ended up on the Scottish coast, but it is a great rarity and a curious sight.

The preserved tentacle club of the giant squid, *Architeuthis dux*, collected by Professor James Ritchie from the Firth of Forth, and (opposite) his painting of the animal from which the club came.

Taking to the land

Westlothiana lizziae lived 345 million years ago. She is believed to be the world's earliest known amniote, an animal with waterproof skin, which lays eggs that can hatch on land.

Finding the specimen was a momentous achievement. This animal was an evolutionary step forward from the first amphibians. Two specimens are known, but this example, discovered in 1984 in East Kirkton Quarry, West Lothian, in central Scotland, was the first and most complete. The creature was nicknamed 'Lizzie the Lizard', as it superficially resembled present-day lizards. However, 'Lizzie' lived over 120 million years before the first lizards, and is actually an animal on the cusp of becoming an early reptile. This lizard-like form was commemorated in the species name as *lizziae*; the genus name *Westlothiana* records where self-taught palaeontologist Stan Wood found the specimen. East Kirkton is an unusual fossil deposit because it represents a vanished ecosystem that included land animals and plants, and also animals living only in water. Regular ash-falls from nearby volcanos into the East Kirkton lake helped to preserve them.

Westlothiana lived about 15 million years after the first four-legged animals emerged from water on to land. If these four-legged (tetrapod) animals had never made this momentous step, the world we know today would not exist. Scotland was then a very different place: lying close to the Equator, hot, humid and subject to droughts and flooding. Here a major evolutionary event occurred: tetrapods, backboned animals with four limbs, moved from water on to land. Yet there was a gap in the fossil record, between 360 and 345 million years ago. No tetrapod fossils had been found from this missing time period; there was no evidence to show how this landmark change had happened.

Many tetrapods are known after this gap, *Westlothiana lizziae* among them. Amphibians were by this stage well adapted to walking on land, with slender limbs and the ability to breathe out of water.

Stan Wood, who found this and many other fossils, and his colleague Tim Smithson, began looking for earlier tetrapod fossils in outcrops of rocks in the Scottish Borders. Eventually, they discovered tetrapod fossils dating from those crucial missing years. Recent excavations have made amazing discoveries, of a new fossilised complete ecosystem alongside unique evidence of early land-based tetrapods.

Gradually, the record is becoming more complete. Will Scotland's rocks now reveal the next part of the story of the evolution of life on land?

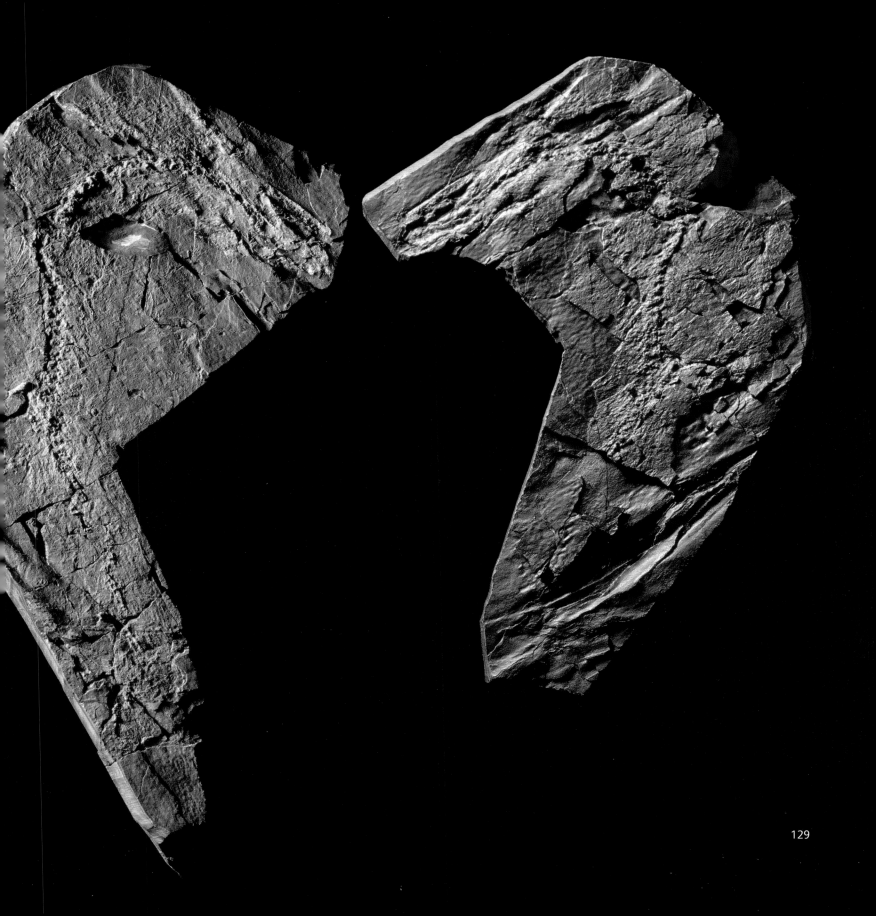

Testimony of the rocks

The statue of Hugh Miller (1802–56) in his outdoors Lowlander Scots dress was carved by Amelia Paton Hill in 1869, ten years after his collection of several thousand fossils was purchased by the Museum. Miller is shown in the act of discovering the fossil fish *Pterichthyodes milleri* on the beach at Cromarty, Ross and Cromarty, in the north of Scotland, his birthplace. The split rock, with the fossil half in his hand and half at his feet, as well as the coarse conglomerate boulder behind him, are all characteristic of this Old Red Sandstone site.

Miller was arguably one of the great founders of geology, and his extensive fossil collection is one of the best early examples. Originally a stonemason, he combined deep religious beliefs with a passion for geology and folklore. Science and religion were intertwined in Hugh Miller's life. From 1839 he became involved in the fierce debates that led to the 1843 Disruption of the Church of Scotland, and the secession of the Free Kirk.

Miller published three books on geology: *The Old Red Sandstone* (1841), *Footprints of the Creator* (1850), and finally *The Testimony of the Rocks* (1856) in the year that he died. His writings were filled with the thrill of discovery and the wonder and beauty of fossils, inspiring future geologists including John Muir (1838–1914), a pioneer of environmental conservation. Miller's travels around Scotland allowed him to visit many fossil-bearing sites, including some difficult to access locations in the Inner Hebrides off the west coast while aboard the yacht *Betsey*.

Pterichthyodes milleri was probably a primitive bottom-dwelling fish that lived during the Devonian Period, 358–416 million years ago. Fossils of its distinctively armoured head and body are relatively common in the Old Red Sandstone of Miller's native area. Another, much larger armoured fish in the Museum's collection, *Homostius milleri*, is also named after him. The extreme divergence of *Pterichthyodes* and *Homostius* from modern-day fish made them a puzzle, unsolved until Charles Darwin published his theories on evolution.

Hugh Miller (above), statue by Amelia Paton Hill, 1869, and the fossil *Pterichthyodes milleri* (opposite), that lived 358–416 million years ago.

Forever amber

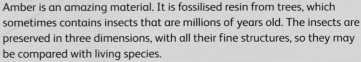

Amber is an amazing material. It is fossilised resin from trees, which sometimes contains insects that are millions of years old. The insects are preserved in three dimensions, with all their fine structures, so they may be compared with living species.

The oldest amber in the Museum collection to contain insects is Burmese amber, and is 99 million years old, originating in the time of the dinosaurs. Amber is dated from the rocks in which it is found. It would have formed from resin on trees that then fell off, to be transported by water and buried under sediments. The Museum's Burmese amber collection is relatively small, but what it contains is special: the first recorded woodlouse (pictured top), for example, named recently as a new species. This species belongs to a very advanced group of woodlice. Previously it was assumed that woodlice evolved and diversified relatively late; this one in amber proves they were already quite highly evolved by 100 million years ago.

There is also a recently named new species of biting midge (middle picture) in the Museum's Burmese amber collection. There has been speculation that some midges in amber may have fed on the blood of dinosaurs; certainly today different species of biting midges feed on the blood of a range of creatures. The 1993 Hollywood movie 'Jurassic Park' popularised the idea of extracting the DNA from blood-sucking insects in amber, with alarming results. The movie was based on seemingly successful attempts to extract insect DNA. Since then, various teams have tried but failed to repeat this research. The original laboratories' samples were probably contaminated with modern insect DNA.

The Museum also has a good collection of Mexican amber, about 15–20 million years old. A rare earwig (pictured below) was recently named as a new species and is the first earwig to be named from Mexican amber.

Amber does not only preserve insects, sometimes it preserves evidence of past insect activity. One specimen from the Museum's Dominican amber collection contains strands of spider silk, a very fragile material, otherwise unknown in the fossil record. What is more, a fairy wasp and gall midge are stuck on the spider's web (background picture), hanging from the threads they were caught in 16 million years ago.

Rock worlds

The oldest evidence in the world of a terrestrial ecosystem, with a variety of animals and plants that all lived together, is found in a truly remarkable rock.

Rhynie Chert is only known from Rhynie, a tiny village in Aberdeen-shire in the north east of Scotland. Individual fossils of distinct animals and plants were known before Rhynie Chert was discovered a century ago, but in this rock there is a diversity of plants and animals that would have interacted with each other. The ecosystem preserved here gives a great insight into what life was like on land in the Early Devonian period, 412 million years ago, long before amphibians crawled out on to the land over 50 million years later.

Chert is made from silica, the same material that glass is made from. Rhynie Chert was formed from hot springs, like those active today in Yellowstone National Park, United States of America, and it is remarkable for preserving the cellular structure of plants.

Primitive plant stems are found in Rhynie Chert, often in the position in which they were growing, and can be clearly observed as black lines in the large polished specimen shown here. Under a microscope their cells can be seen, perfectly preserved.

Within this rock world are very primitive plants called club mosses – small branching plants that are still living today, although rare. There are also small animals, including primitive spiders and the earliest known fossil insects in the world.

Two insect species have been found in Rhynie Chert. The first, *Rhyniella praecursor*, is a springtail, a primitive group of insects. The second, *Rhyniognatha hirsti*, identified by a pair of jaws, was recognised by American scientists in the 1990s. These jaws were similar to those of a mayfly, although the insect was almost certainly without wings. The insects would have developed feeding strategies before the need to fly: the first fossil evidence of flying insects is about 80 million years later.

The state of preservation within the rock is truly remarkable – modern-day springs in Yellowstone and New Zealand also preserve plant stems, but not as well as in Rhynie Chert. It is not known how the cells became so perfectly preserved.

Crystals of gold

Gold can be found as either veins in rocks or as loose nuggets on the surface of the Earth. Nuggets often have a rounded, water-worn appearance but sometimes occur as distinct crystals. There are examples of both types in the collections of the Museum, but this specimen, known as the 'Liversidge Nugget', comprises a group of fine crystals of gold.

The nugget is originally thought to be from Ballarat in the State of Victoria in Australia; however, comparisons with specimens in other collections have cast doubt on this. Nevertheless Ballarat, and the surrounding area, is one of the most famous gold-mining areas in the world. Its discovery in 1851 triggered a massive gold-rush, but unlike other gold-rushes, mining continued in Victoria until very recently.

Details of how, when and why this specimen ended up in the collections of this Museum have been lost. It was registered in 1921, but it is known to have been in the Museum in 1876 and this is where the link with Liversidge comes in.

London-born Archibald Liversidge (1847–1927) was educated at the Royal College of Chemistry, the Royal School of Mines and Christ's College, Cambridge. In 1872 he was offered a post at the University of Sydney, becoming Professor of Geology in 1874. In 1876 he published his seminal work on Australian mineralogy, *The Minerals of New South Wales*. In this important survey, Liversidge featured the nugget in images and words, describing it as 'a beautiful group of gold crystals … seen in the Museum of Science and Art in Edinburgh – perhaps one of the finest in existence'. A later portrait of Liversidge, hanging in the University of Sydney, shows him holding the nugget, or a model of the nugget sent to him by the Director of this Museum at the time, Professor Thomas Archer.

Over the years, through exhibitions and publications, the connection between the nugget and Liversidge has strengthened and the two have become inextricably linked.

Specimens of this quality are rare and the Museum is proud to have it in the collections.

Sky fall

On 3 December 1917, an elderly couple, Mr and Mrs Thomas Hill, were sitting at home in the South Lodge of the Keithick Estate in Perthshire when they heard a loud bang on the roof. Thinking it might be a falling branch they went outside and saw a hole in the roof. Their daughter, Mary Hill, clambered up and looked into the hole and could see a large rock sitting on one of the joists. The next morning a tradesman was called to repair the damage. He recovered the rock and sealed the hole.

The mystery rock was first examined by Henry Coates of the Perthshire Society of Natural Science. It was then forwarded to the Museum, where it was identified as a meteorite. By that time another three pieces had come to light. Many people in eastern Scotland and northern England had witnessed the meteorite blazing a trail through the sky. The four fragments together make the largest known Scottish meteorite – the Strathmore Meteorite.

The Keithick fragment weighed a little over 2 kilograms; if it had not lodged in the roof joists, it would have crashed through the ceiling into the room below. The largest piece, the Easter Essendy fragment, which is also in the Museum's collection, weighed over 9 kilograms.

Meteorites are not rare. There are three basic types: iron meteorites, composed entirely of metal; stony meteorites, largely composed of minerals that you would find in rocks on Earth; and stony iron, a mixture of the two. The Strathmore meteorite is a stony meteorite (chondrite), the most common type.

It is assumed by many that meteorites are hot when they reach Earth. When they pass through the atmosphere they generate a fireball as friction heats up and melts the outer surface. However, the heat is soon lost and when they reach the ground they may be no hotter than the ambient temperature. They can, however, be very cold. The bodies that become meteorites spend millions of years in deep space, where it is just above absolute zero (−273°C). The few seconds spent as a fireball is not enough to heat the whole meteor so that its very cold core remains unheated.

Atomic number 38

The element strontium (symbol Sr) was first discovered in mineral specimens from Scotland. It is named after the place where it was found, the small former mining town of Strontian on the Ardnamurchan peninsula in Argyll in the west of Scotland.

The town of Strontian – the smallest place to have an element named after it – only came into existence with the start of lead mining in 1722. The landowner built the town on a bay of Loch Sunart to accommodate the miners and their families, to process the ore and to provide a safe harbour to ship the processed ore out. Though lead ore was the primary target, over time many different and useful minerals were found and extracted. One of these was baryte – sometimes called 'heavy spar' at that time. Lead mining at Strontian eventually ceased in the early part of the 20th century, but baryte mining continued until the 1980s when the last mine closed down.

In the late 1780s samples from Strontian were acquired by Dr Adair Crawford, a Northern Irish doctor working in London, and his Scottish assistant William Cruickshank, who were together researching the medicinal properties of baryte. Crawford and Cruickshank realised that some of the material from Strontian was quite different from baryte. The work was published in 1790, declaring that the mineral contained '… a new species of earth [element] which has not hitherto been sufficiently examined'. Other scientists, in Germany, Britain and Ireland, also working on material from Strontian, came to a similar conclusion. In 1808 Sir Humphrey Davy successfully isolated the element, naming it 'strontium'.

Pure strontium is a pale green to silvery-grey metal. It is extremely reactive with oxygen and water, which means it only occurs naturally when combined with other elements. It has been used in applications such as the production of sugar from sugar beet, fireworks (it produces a vivid red colour) and television cathode-ray tube manufacture.

In 1791, the German scientist F G Sulzer published a paper in which he described a new mineral from Strontian which he called 'strontianit' ('strontianite' in English). In his paper he also noted that this new mineral contained a new element confirming the earlier work of Crawford and Cruickshank.

'God's Treasure House'

Scotland's most famous mineral and metal mining region is in the Lowther Hills in the Southern Uplands, centred on the villages of Leadhills and Wanlockhead. It is the 'type locality' (where the mineral species were first discovered) for ten mineral species.

Three of these minerals are lanarkite (opposite), which was named after the county of Lanarkshire; leadhillite after the village of Leadhills; and susannite (right) after the Susanna Vein which ran north-west of the village of Leadhills. All are forms of lead sulphate often displaying beautiful crystal forms and vivid colours. The type specimens (the specimens that were first used to describe the new species) are housed in the Muséum national d'histoire naturelle in Paris. First recognised in 1813 by French scientist René Just Haüy in the collections of the Comte Jacque Louis de Bournon, they were given their current names by another French scientist, Francois Beudant in 1832.

The rich products of the mines led to the area being called 'God's Treasure House in Scotland'. The first written historical record of mining is from 1239, when King David I of Scotland granted a charter to the monks of Newbattle Abbey to mine the area for gold. The fine gold produced there was used to make some of Scotland's currency and part of the Scottish crown jewels in the 16th century. When gold was effectively exhausted, mining for lead followed, which also produced silver as the lead ore, galena, was silver-rich.

Although many relics of old mine workings and dumps remain, it is difficult now to gauge the great extent of the mining that went on. Individual workings were often on a small scale. With such a hilly location, near some of the highest villages in Scotland, working there in winter must have been difficult. All mining effectively ended in the 1950s; the seams were exhausted and the mines became more difficult to work.

This small, remote area has had a long history of mining – over 700 years. The mines of Leadhills and Wanlockhead produced high quality gold and half a million tons of lead. The number of minerals found at this locality is phenomenal, including the examples pictured here and many others. It was indeed a metal and mineral treasure house.

Hunted to extinction

Georg Wilhelm Steller (1709–46) was the naturalist on the Great Northern Expedition to the Pacific coast of Siberia in 1741. This was led by Vitus Bering, a Danish explorer in Russian service, after whom the Straits between Russia and Alaska are named. Bering and many of his companions were stranded and died on this trip, but Steller and his shipmates survived by eating the flesh of the sea cow. The sea cow was named after Steller, who first recorded it.

An enormous marine mammal up to 9 metres in length, the sea cow (*Hydrodamalis gigas*) fed on kelp, a kind of seaweed. It is related to the dugong and manatee, and some called it the bark animal because of its very thick skin which protected it from being buffeted against the rocks. Animals like these also have very dense rib bones, to help counteract the buoyancy of their lungs, and so they have neutral buoyancy.

Others followed where Bering and Steller had led. They were motivated to venture into the Arctic and north Pacific waters to hunt sea otters for fur, but oil was also needed for burning in lamps. The sea cows, a valuable source of oil, were easily caught as they could not swim fast. They were exploited ruthlessly for their oil, for their skins to make boats, and their flesh, which made good eating. Within just 27 years of their discovery, the Steller's sea cow had become extinct.

Skeletal remains of this animal are very rare, being found in only a few museums. This skull and other bones were collected by Sir D'Arcy Wentworth Thompson (1860–1948), a pioneer in mathematical biology. He was famous for his 1917 book *On Growth and Form*, which looked at the mathematical basis for shape and transformations of shape in animals and plants. In 1896–97 he went to the Bering Straits as part of an international inquiry into the fur seal industry. There he uncovered the bones of Steller's sea cow on Copper Island, which were transported back to Dundee Zoology Museum. In the 1950s, when that museum was reduced in size, the skeleton came to Edinburgh.

The complete skeleton is very fragile and only the skull can be put on display, but even from the skull it is apparent how large and imposing Steller's sea cows actually were. A cast of a complete skeleton can be found in the Wildlife Panorama in the Museum's Natural World galleries.

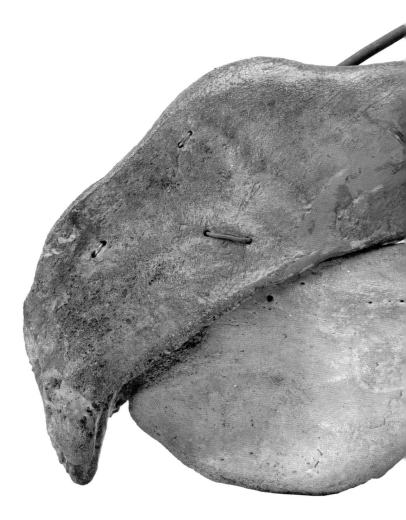

Moby on the Forth

'Moby' was the nickname given to the first sperm whale for 200 years to be beached in the Firth of Forth, the estuary between Fife and Lothian in Scotland. The whale had been present in the Forth for about a week during March 1997, but numerous attempts to guide him back out to the open sea failed. Eventually he died and was towed ashore at a slipway near Airth in the Falkirk area. The event captured the imagination of local people, and the press gave the animal his nickname, after the whale in Herman Melville's novel *Moby Dick*.

The Museum has one of the largest and finest research collections of marine mammals in the world, used to help curators and others understand these remarkable animals. Skeletons from the larger whales were at one time obtained through the Scottish whaling industry, but nowadays the Museum relies on beached animals that have died naturally, as in the case of Moby.

Museum staff initially intended to examine and measure the animal on the beach, but ended up adding the whole skeleton to the collection. First of all, the local council had to deal with the dead whale. The animal was put on to the back of a lorry with the help of two mobile cranes; it was then taken to the council landfill waste site in nearby Bo'ness, West Lothian, where Museum staff were able to work on it.

The practical problems associated with this task were immense. Staff had to deal with a whale carcass that was about 15 metres long and 40 tonnes in weight, using only knives to avoid damaging the bones. Staff donned waterproof suits and rubber boots, working as fast as possible because the carcass was putrefying rapidly.

Once the carcass had been dismembered, the bones were extracted and brought back to the Museum's facilities in Edinburgh. It took another six weeks to prepare the skeleton from the roughly cleaned bones, before the skull of Moby finally went on display.

Moby tasted fame once again in 2009 when the skull was loaned to the Glasgow-based Turner Prize nominee Lucy Skaer for her work *Leviathan Edge 2009* at Tate Britain in London.

The last survivor

The quagga (*Equus quagga*) is an unusual extinct zebra with very few stripes. It has striping on the head and neck, with sometimes a little on the body, and it was a distinct species which is now extinct. The quagga's name was given to it by the Boer colonists of the Cape of Good Hope, and it comes from its distinctive call, 'kwa-ha', the same call as fully-striped plains zebras from elsewhere in Africa.

The quagga had long been hunted for its meat and skin; by 1878 the animal was extinct in the wild. The last zoo specimen died in Amsterdam five years later.

This Museum possesses a very special quagga: the only one ever photographed alive. She arrived at London Zoo in 1858 and died in 1872; her mounted skin came to Edinburgh in 1879, but her skeleton is in Yale University in the United States.

There was at one time some doubt as to whether the mounted skin in this Museum did indeed belong to the quagga in the famous photograph featured here, but each zebra has a unique striping pattern. Painstaking checks confirmed that she was indeed the same one.

In 1984, the quagga was the first extinct animal to have its DNA analysed, using tissue samples taken from museum specimens. Genetically it is very similar to the plains zebra; but it is at the opposite end of the spectrum from fully striped zebras found in east Africa. In the Quagga Project in South Africa, animals with the least striping were bred with each other to create zebras that look like quaggas. These have been 'reintroduced' on to their former range.

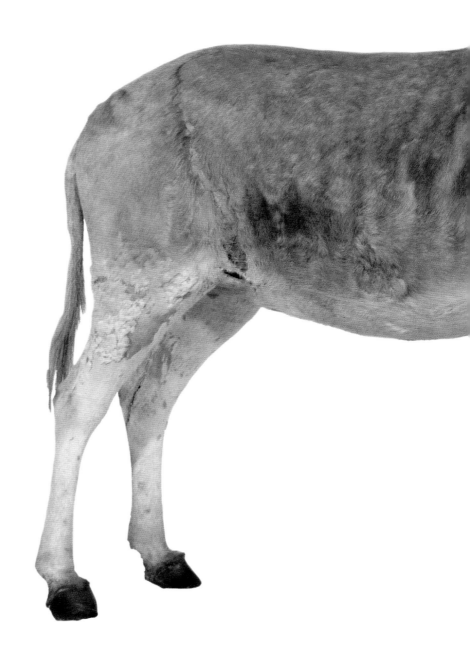

Quagga mare at London Zoo in 1870.

Panda diplomacy

The giant panda Ching Ching (1972–85) and her partner Chia Chia were a gift to Britain from the Chinese government in 1974, following Prime Minister Edward Heath's visit there. During the Cold War, the People's Republic of China presented several countries with pandas, in what came to be known as 'panda diplomacy'. Their rarity gave them special status, as the giant panda (*Ailuropoda melanoleuca*) is one of the world's most endangered animal species. There are now thought to be just over 1800 left in China, mostly in the mountain areas of the south west, and their natural forest habitat is threatened by encroaching agriculture and a growing human population.

Ching Ching was a great draw at London Zoo. A giant panda's colouration is distinctive and its cute teddy-bear looks help to make it popular. There was also continuing international interest in whether she would have cubs, given the difficulty in breeding pandas in captivity.

In evolutionary terms giant pandas are fascinating because they are carnivores that have adapted largely for feeding on bamboo. They have very powerful jaw muscles, massive teeth, and a high vaulted skull for the jaw muscles to attach to. They also have a wrist bone that has become adapted to give a grip that can hold bamboo stems: the so-called panda's thumb.

Visitors are always interested in seeing giant pandas. The Museum was fortunate to be given Ching Ching after she died, and has placed her and one other panda on display. They are a particular focus for discussion of conservation and the plight of endangered species, not least because the giant panda is itself the emblem of the World Wide Fund for Nature.

Above all, perhaps, Ching Ching had a political importance. She was one of the last giant pandas donated to the United Kingdom, rather than being sent on loan as is now the case with Chinese pandas. She was a symbol of a great gift between nations.

Ching Ching eating a mouthful of bamboo shoots at London Zoo.

Revolutionary theory

A mounted bird, with a ragged label on the base, appears an insufficient token for one of the greatest scientific lives, that of Charles Darwin (1809–82), from whose collection this specimen originated. Yet it was from close and detailed observation of the variety of life, whether around the world or in his own garden, that led to his great theory of evolution by natural selection.

A carved portrait of Darwin, probably the world's best-known naturalist, is one of the four heads above the former main entrance doors of the Museum. Darwin had studied medicine in Edinburgh between 1825 and 1827, and his lodgings were in a building very close to this Museum. The vast natural history collections of the University of Edinburgh were a unique resource for an aspiring naturalist and Darwin acquired many skills here – anatomy, collecting, recording and skinning – which he used throughout his career. Indeed, he learned his skinning skills from a former slave, John Edmonstone, from Guyana, a taxidermist in Edinburgh.

Later, after graduating from Cambridge, Darwin was given a life-changing opportunity to become the naturalist on the scientific survey of the southern hemisphere aboard HMS *Beagle*. Between 1831 and 1836, he explored places around the globe, collecting animal and plant specimens.

Darwin collected 468 bird skins on the *Beagle* voyage. This scaly-throated earthcreeper (*Upucerthia dumetaria*) was shot, probably by his assistant Syms Covington, in Chile in April or May 1835, on a journey into the interior from the port city of Coquimbo. Covington had probably collected other examples of this species in Argentina two years before, but there were subtle differences between these birds from either side of the Andes.

Two years later Darwin reached the momentous conclusion that species were neither fixed nor created by miracle, but had evolved. He was convinced by reflection on the numerous observations and the substantial specimen collections made on the *Beagle* voyage. In 1859, he published his work on natural selection, *On the Origin of Species*. Through the scaly-throated earthcreeper and a myriad of other animals, Darwin revolutionised the way in which humans think about themselves and the natural world.

Tools for the task

The New Caledonian crow (*Corvus moneduloides*) is a remarkable bird; not for its appearance, as it looks rather like a jackdaw, but because it has an incredible ability to make all kinds of tools for obtaining its food – one of which looks rather like a cricket bat.

The bird is confined to New Caledonia, an island in the south-west Pacific Ocean. Scientists have been studying this crow for many years. It has become a model in trying to understand how the making and use of tools affects the evolution of intelligence. In experiments the birds have proved capable of solving sophisticated cognitive tests. These crows are constantly active, even frenetic, looking for something to do; presumably their tool-making ability keeps their large brains occupied.

Making tools out of spines, twigs and leaves, a bird will use its chosen tool to grub out insect larvae from rotting wood by holding it in its beak, then skewering and pulling. Some of the tools have hooks on the end – either twigs fashioned by the bird or chosen for their natural barbs.

Tool-making is not unique, even among birds, but it is the array and the complexity of tools – and the fact that the crows learn from each other how to create them – which make New Caledonian crows very special.

Research with captive birds is being undertaken at the University of Oxford by Professor Alex Kacelnick and his team, who supplied the Museum with this crow. Determined also to obtain a genuine tool made by a crow in New Caledonia, even though it may look just like a twig, the Museum persisted in its quest. One duly arrived. This very special twig from 9917 miles away is registered separately within the collections, with its exact collecting locality.

Science and Technology

Technology was at the heart of the Museum from its very inception. The founding industrial collection reflected Scotland's role as one of the world's economic powerhouses, at the forefront of technological progress.

Curators continued to collect the technology of the day, and in the 20th century expanded the collections to include science. The chronological range of the artefacts also expanded as curators acquired older treasures, and the original collections themselves became valuable as historic artefacts. Today the Museum's collecting continues this rich blend of classic and cutting-edge, applied technology and pure science.

The Scottish contribution to understanding the universe can be seen from the intricate apparatus of Enlightenment chemistry to a recent Nobel Prize. The Museum also reveals our fascination with the human body, whether to understand anatomy or to identify and treat disease.

Scotland is a nation of pragmatic problem-solvers. The collections therefore reflect the processes, tools and materials of engineering and manufacturing, communication technologies and networks, innovation in design, and the sources and generation of the energy we use.

The Museum is especially famous for its precision model-making, enabling the display of items that were too large, too far away, or too dangerous to show at Chambers Street. Outsized industrial machinery, lighthouses on distant rocks, or massive civil engineering have been reduced in scale and exhibited to delight and to educate.

Alongside the models, of course, are originals: the first pneumatic bicycle tyre and the first carbon-fibre bicycle, a vast steam engine for pumping water and a tiny motor that powers a bionic hand, a glider and a performance racing car, an adding machine and a smartphone, a tiny dynamo and a giant wind turbine blade. All are collected for what they can tell us about innovation in design, the application of technology and the power of invention.

Curators continue to work with scientists – prize-winners in the making – to acquire new objects. In this way, trailblazing Scottish science and technology can continue to inspire the Museum's visitors, and the next wave of innovators of the future.

Dolly the sheep

She may look like any other sheep, but she is cutting-edge biotechnology in sheep's clothing. She is a celebrity and has been since she was born. Although she is a clone, she is unique. She is Dolly.

A clone has the same DNA sequence as its parent; they are genetically identical. Dolly was created at the Roslin Institute, now part of the University of Edinburgh, by Professor Ian Wilmut and his team, including Bill Ritchie who carried out the delicate task of cloning the sheep that would become Dolly. Several earlier clones had been produced in the lab, from DNA taken from embryos. Dolly is remarkable in being the first mammal to be cloned from an adult cell. A major scientific achievement, she demonstrated that a nucleus from an adult cell, despite being differentiated for a specific function – in this case a sheep's udder – may be used to create an entire organism.

Dolly had three mothers; a Scottish Blackface ewe provided the egg; the DNA came from an udder cell of a Finn Dorset sheep; and another Scottish Blackface carried the cloned embryo. From 277 original cell fusions, only one pregnancy went to full term, and the 6.6 kilogram Finn Dorset lamb 6LLS was born on 5 July 1996. Dolly. Her existence was announced the following February, and media interest exploded.

Dolly lived a pampered existence at the Roslin Institute. Unlike other sheep, she was so accustomed to close human contact that she approached visitors rather than running away. Dolly mated and produced six normal offspring, showing that cloned animals are capable of reproducing. Well cared-for and living indoors most of her life, Dolly was also overweight, and suffered from arthritis and an incurable lung tumour. She was put to sleep on 14 February 2003, aged six and a half.

Within months of Dolly's birth, the Roslin Institute agreed that the Museum could preserve and display Dolly after her death. A contingency plan ensured that when the time came, a taxidermy team was ready to collect Dolly and prepare her for posterity. Within hours of her death, she was in the Museum's possession. Cloning and genetic manipulation continues, but nothing can reproduce Dolly's iconic status.

Powered up

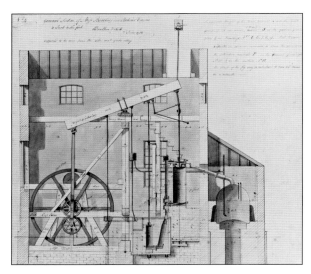

A drawing (No. 4) by James Watt, the original design for the Boulton and Watt engine in the Museum's collection.

Thomas Newcomen built the first working steam engine in 1712 and his design remained the most efficient way of pumping water from mines for 50 years.

In 1765, while repairing a working Newcomen model at the University of Edinburgh, James Watt (1736–1819) realised that it wasted a lot of steam and power. This was because steam came into the engine cylinder at high temperature and was cooled, causing the cylinder to alternate between hot and cold.

It is said that Watt had a 'eureka moment' while out walking on Glasgow Green, when he realised that if a separate condensing area were to be added, then the cylinder would not be heated and cooled with every cycle, making the whole process more efficient. He called the steam cooling chamber a 'condenser' and patented his invention in 1769.

Built in 1786, this monumental 9.5-metre-high engine is the result of a partnership between James Watt and businessman Matthew Boulton. Watt provided the technical and engineering knowledge for the engine, while Boulton supplied money and business expertise to manufacture Watt's inventions. This engine was installed in the Barclay & Perkins brewery in Southwark, London, and with some minor modifications it was used to pump water and grind barley for almost a hundred years. The engine uses 'sun and planet' gears which allow the up and down pumping motion to be to be changed into rotary motion.

Boulton and Watt patented their developments for 25 years, giving them a head start on the competition. They had one of the most successful partnerships of the Industrial Revolution and their engines were used all over the United Kingdom and further afield.

This engine was acquired by the Museum in 1886, just a year after it came out of service in London, and was installed in its current location in 2006. Visitors can still see it in action at the Museum today.

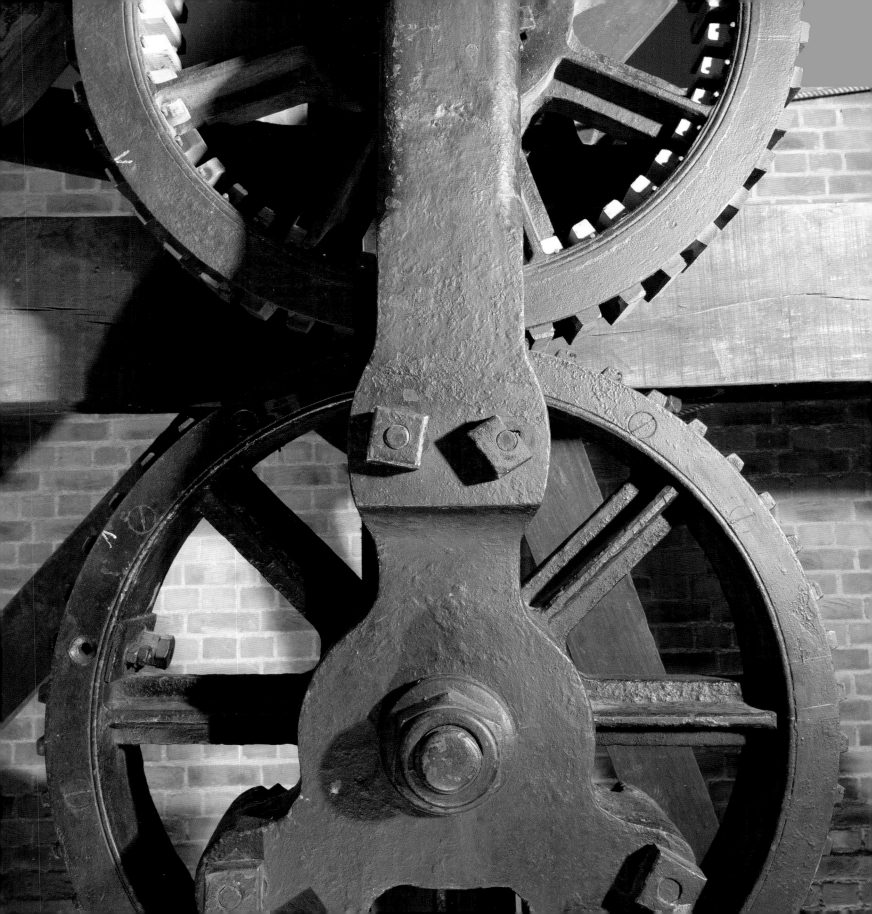

First flights

The *Hawk* glider in the Museum is the oldest surviving British aeroplane. Percy Pilcher (1866–99) constructed it in 1896, with his sister Ella, during his time as an assistant in the Department of Naval Architecture at the University of Glasgow. This was one of several aircraft that he built, all with names of flying creatures – *Bat*, *Beetle*, *Gull* and *Hawk*.

Pilcher was in correspondence with many contemporary pioneer aviators, including the Wright brothers in the United States, swapping knowledge on ideas and experiments.

The glider was made out of bamboo, wire and a very finely woven cotton fabric called nainsook. Ella possibly did much of the sewing and helped with the overall construction. To make it as air-resistant as possible, the cloth was treated with a liquid compound, probably containing lead.

The *Hawk* glider was built in Glasgow in the west of Scotland, and was designed so that the wings could be folded for transportation. Pilcher flew some of his gliders above Dunbartonshire, west of the city.

Pilcher had his eye on powered flight and was developing a glider with a small engine. Unable to demonstrate it due to a broken crankshaft, Pilcher took the *Hawk* out during an event at Stanford Hall in Leicestershire, England, on 30 September 1899. Because he had not fully understood the effect of gust-loads on the tail-planes, the tail broke in bad weather and the glider crashed heavily. Pilcher died two days later.

This glider had a chequered history after that. It became part of a collection of early aeroplanes at the Royal Aero-nautical Society, London, and has been on loan to the Museum since 1909. In the 1960s the original dilapidated fabric was replaced, and it has recently been replaced again in a more authentic way.

Is it still flyable? There are replicas of the *Hawk*, and in the 1960s a well-known glider pilot, Derek Piggott, flew one. Nowadays they all remain grounded.

Freddy the robot

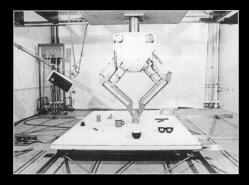

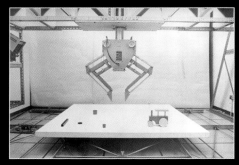

Freddy the robot with objects for it to identify, at the University of Edinburgh, early 1970s.

Freddy was the first robot to combine a 'seeing' eye – two video cameras – with a tactile hand or gripper. It was developed in the University of Edinburgh's Department of Machine Intelligence and Perception from 1969. It could see and feel what it was doing, at a time when almost all other robots were working by blind reckoning, moving objects from one known position to another a fixed distance away. Freddy was a true pioneer, a milestone in artificial intelligence, and has been preserved for posterity. It may not be particularly polished in appearance, but it did its job well.

The experimenters had videoed children aged about three assembling two toys: a model car and a sailing boat. They then set Freddy up and programmed it to do these tasks. The robot's hand stays still and a large platform holding the objects moves around underneath. That was an easier solution than having the gripper move. Working glacially slowly, Freddy took all night to perform the task. The researchers tipped out the contents of a toy box. It would pick up the parts, lay them out and look at them individually. Taking up to 20 minutes to analyse an image and identify it, Freddy would then pick up the piece, put it in order and add it to the assembly. It could cope with failure, and see if it had picked something up or had missed it. It would certainly notice if the researchers started to change things round, and would demand the return of objects taken away.

There were two Freddy robots. The first was built in 1969 and Freddy II, which is the version in the Museum, was an upgrade in the early 1970s. Freddy was made from everyday items – metal shelving, strip lights, television cameras – and two powerful computers. One small computer, only the size of two or three filing cabinets, was in the same room as the robot and handled image processing. The other, larger, one had a room to itself and transmitted data through electricity cables.

Freddy looks like something people might make when they are experimenting, but it is a pioneer in artificial intelligence. All cutting-edge engineering technology projects tend to acquire a name and personality, and this one even seems to have a face.

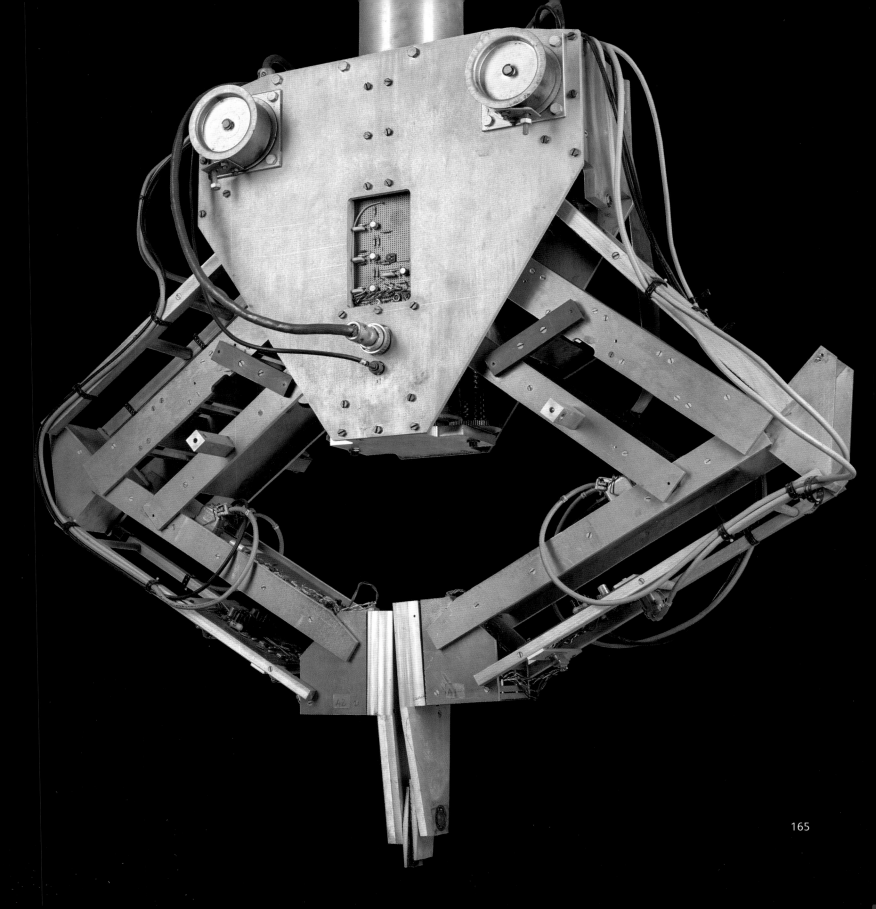

A head of steam

Wylam Dilly is one of two sister engines that are, together, the earliest steam locomotives in the world. The other is *Puffing Billy*, now in the Science Museum in London. Designed by William Hedley (1779–1843) and built in 1813, they were used to haul coal at the Wylam Colliery in County Durham in north-east England. The Museum's locomotive is named after the colliery, and a 'dilly' is a coal-waggon.

The locomotive has wheels 5 feet apart and originally ran on a plateway – flat plates with inner edges to keep the wheels in place. But it did not stay that way for long. In 1822 the men who took coal from the end of the plateway, down the River Tyne on flat boats called keels, went on strike. Hedley had *Wylam Dilly* converted into a tugboat to haul the keels down-river, ending the Keelmen's strike. Later the wheels were re-attached, and in around 1830 were converted again when wrought-iron rails were laid to replace the plateway.

Wylam Dilly had a single-tube boiler with a large diameter, which was the most efficient of its time. The multi-tube boiler came in later with George Stephenson's *Rocket*, giving it a much more efficient engine. *Rocket* famously won the Rainhill steam locomotive trials in October 1829 for the Liverpool and Manchester Railway.

As *Wylam Dilly* had a very long life, working for 54 years, it must have been effective enough in use. An investigation of *Wylam Dilly* today shows that there were a number of changes made during the locomotive's working life, so experimentation was clearly undertaken to improve its performance.

The railway engine is an icon of the modern age, and to have the joint-first engine is very important. *Wylam Dilly* came to the Museum directly in 1882 from the Hedley family who had owned the colliery. Since its arrival it has only been off display twice, when it was loaned to international exhibitions in the 19th century.

Scottish air

Johnny Dunlop on his bicycle with new pneumatic tyres, developed by his father in 1888.

In 1910, John Boyd Dunlop presented to the Museum the oldest bicycle pneumatic tyre in the world. Today our road transport infrastructure and many other things would be very different without this invention.

The name of John Boyd Dunlop (1840–1921) is forever associated with the pneumatic tyre, although it was originally invented by Robert Thompson from Stonehaven in Aberdeenshire, north-east Scotland. Thompson patented a multi-tube design for possible use on horse-drawn vehicles in 1845, but he never developed the idea. When Dunlop created his design in 1888, he claimed to know nothing of Thompson.

Born in Ayrshire in south-west Scotland, Dunlop was running a veterinary practice in Belfast at the time of his invention. His son Johnny was a sickly boy who had difficulty riding his tricycle on solid rubber tyres, and Dunlop wanted to make his life more comfortable. To this end he began experimenting in the yard behind his premises, rolling wheels of different designs down the cobbled surface to see what worked best. In this way he came up with the concept of an air-filled tyre.

Dunlop tried to persuade several companies to make his tyre, but they thought the idea unworkable. Finally a prototype was made in Edinburgh by Thornton a rubber goods manufacturer, using Arbroath sailcloth as the base material. Dunlop tried it out on his son's bicycle – both the front and back wheel – with great success.

The back wheel was sent to France in support of a patent application, but was lost, so the front is the only one that has survived.

At the 1890 Stanley Bicycle Show in London, 20 bicycles out of 1500 on display had pneumatic tyres. Two years later only three used solid tyres. Sales of the pneumatic tyre took off very rapidly and Dunlop set up factories in Ireland and Germany, which provided many of them.

This was also perfect timing for the motor car, as Carl Benz's first automobile ran in 1886. Despite Dunlop's invention, some early motorists still preferred to use a solid tyre because of the frequent punctures caused by horseshoe tacks on the road. But the pneumatic tyre was there, ready to roll in the future.

Lean mean machine

Carbon fibre was a new material, incredibly strong and light, at the time Mike Burrows designed his revolutionary bicycle in 1985. It enabled him to make a very stiff but highly aerodynamic bicycle for track racing.

Mike Burrows (b.1943) is one of the most inventive of all bicycle designers, with many successful and innovative designs to his name. His earlier track-race bicycles, which gave the rider a very low profile, were made with steel tubing.

The bicycle in the Museum's collection is the world's first carbon-fibre *monocoque*, a French word for a structure in which the shell bears most of the stress. Made in a mould, the machine is hollow and all in one piece, and therefore stiff, ideal for the track. Racing cyclists do not want a frame that is going to bend, but one that is particularly aerodynamic, and a moulded shape provides this.

Burrows also designed the carbon-fibre Lotus 108 Individual Pursuit bicycle on which British speed cyclist Chris Boardman won a gold medal in the 1992 Barcelona Olympics. Burrows then went on to work with the largest bicycle manufacturer in the world, Giant of Taiwan, and together they made production-line bicycles in carbon fibre.

The Museum has another object that demonstrates Burrows' inventiveness in this material: a monoblade front fork, which was tried out on the bicycle of Scottish cyclist Graeme Obree around the time that he broke the World One Hour record in 1993. Obree, however, did not like the new component because it creaked and groaned – characteristic of the material – and so he went back to a conventional fork.

Mike Burrows gave his original carbon-fibre bicycle to the Cycle Museum in Harlow, Essex. When that collection was dispersed, this Museum applied for a number of bicycles and was pleased to be allocated Burrows' machine. The bicycle has a special place in the Museum's collection because it demonstrates so many different techniques and design principles, as well as being a pioneering object and a visual delight.

Turn of speed

Robert Wilson (1803–82), a native of Dunbar, east of Edinburgh, and the son of a fisherman, was a pioneer of the double screw propeller. A great experimenter, he built this demonstration piece in 1826 to show the superiority of his invention over paddle wheels.

Powered by clockwork, the example now in the Museum's collection had paddles as well as a double screw propeller, to show the Admiralty of the British government that the latter was the more efficient of the two. Apparently inspired by a windmill, Wilson had applied the rotation technique to marine propulsion. At sea, the great advantage of Wilson's new double screw propeller was that it was always in the water; paddles, on the other hand, were a less efficient design – when the ship rolled, one paddle would often be out of the water.

There were others working along similar lines, so it is not certain that Wilson's is the first-ever double screw propeller, but it was he who tried to convince the Admiralty of its worth. In demonstrating how the double screw propeller could be used to power ships, he experimented with different shapes and forms, set at various angles, or with differing numbers of blades. Despite further successful trials with a larger boat at Leith, the port north-east of the capital, the Admiralty did not accept Wilson's concept at that time.

Since Wilson failed initially to persuade the Admiralty, Francis Pettit Smith, a farmer from Kent, England, took up the challenge in 1835 and successfully applied for the first patent. Wilson meanwhile became a celebrated engineer and inventor of steam hammers and other heavy industrial tools. Finally, in 1880, after the development of torpedoes and shortly before his death, the War Office recognised the effectiveness of Wilson's pioneering double screw propeller with a payment of £500.

Wilson's demonstration piece eventually went into the collections of the Highland and Agricultural Society of Scotland, which collected many experimental objects such as ploughs and engines. The Society's collections eventually came to this Museum.

Stitches in time

Sitting on a mahogany base, compact, in brass and wood, is one of the first six sewing machines ever produced. Invented and patented by Elias Howe in Massachusetts, North America, in 1846, it was the first successful lock-stitching machine and the beginning of a domestic industrial revolution that enabled people to sew garments, mechanically, at home. This particular machine was not produced in Scotland, but the patent helped to establish the industry here. The American-owned Singer Machine Company's complex, built in 1873 at Kilbowie, Clydebank, Scotland, was the biggest sewing-machine factory in the world.

A sewing machine is effectively a very small textile mill. Many people in the mid-19th century had been looking at how to mechanise sewing. Howe's stroke of genius was to make the needle with the eye at the point, so it works as a miniature loom – lifting one thread, then shooting the other one through, like a shuttle on a small scale – with an automatic feed of the thread.

Howe's machine is so complex and well engineered, it almost looks like a scientific instrument. It is not how we might picture a sewing machine. Yet this is arguably one of the world's most important innovations, and it is still changing how we produce textiles at home.

Howe's machine was a prototype and too expensive to produce in this form; more experimentation was required. In 1851 Isaac Merritt Singer invented the first practical sewing machine for domestic use. Although made from easily manufactured cast-iron components and thus cheaper and built to last, Singer lost a patent infringement suit brought by Howe in 1854 and the machines were licensed under Howe's patent.

Howe eventually sold his British patent to William Frederick Thomas in Cheapside, London, who turned the nascent business into a major enterprise. Elias Howe was more of an inventor than an entrepreneur. His story shows that commercial success requires not only genius, but an eye for the market, and the ability to translate both into producing something that sells.

The Wright stuff

Wilbur and Orville Wright in 1909.

Orville Wright (1871–1948) and his brother Wilbur (1867–1912) were aviation pioneers who first designed and flew a heavier-than-air powered aircraft. Their successful maiden flight happened on 17 December 1903 above the flat plains of Kitty Hawk, North Carolina in the United States. Wind, sand and a dream of flight had brought the brothers to that location, and after four years of experiments their dreams came true.

The Wright brothers were not the only pioneers to realise that one of the ways to get an aircraft to fly was to build a very light engine; they were, however, the first to achieve success. Car engines of the time were heavy and crudely engineered, so the Wrights' engine was specifically designed for an aeroplane. They used a considerable amount of aluminium in the construction – the crank case, the solders – and it has a very light-weight tin sump on the underside. It was much lighter, but perhaps much less reliable in the long term than a car engine. However, the Wright brothers only contemplated fairly short flights at that time. Although their experiments continued and diversified, the brothers produced essentially the same aero-engine for a while.

In the 1920s, the Museum's Thomas Rowatt was already commissioning models of early planes, including Louis Blériot's successful cross-Channel flying machine. With British aviation pioneer Percy Pilcher's experimental *Hawk* glider already in the collections, Rowatt wrote to Orville Wright requesting an original Wright aero-engine. Orville responded positively by letter, commenting that he and his brother Wilbur were delighted to donate a 1910 engine from a Wright Model B.

The engine and the letter are founding elements of the Museum's world-class aviation collection.

Motorbiking

Colonel Sir Henry Capel Lofft Holden (1856–1937) is perhaps best known today as the designer of the Brooklands race track. In 1907, this was the first purpose-built motor circuit in the United Kingdom. A decade earlier, Holden developed the first motorcycle made in the United Kingdom.

In 1895 Holden took a Crypto-Bantam small-wheeled pedal bicycle and extended the frame. He made his own 1000cc 4-cylinder petrol engine – believed to be the first such petrol engine in the world – and put this into the extended frame to create a motor-cycle. The engine drove the rear wheel through rods and cranks, and was started using the existing pedals on the front wheel.

How safe was this machine? It had very limited braking as it relied on the bicycle's original mechanism of a small rubber pad rubbing on the front tyre. Its top-speed of 25 miles an hour must have been alarming on a small-wheeled bicycle.

The prototype was crude, but it demonstrated the principle enough for Holden to go on to make a small number of production machines, of which there are just two in existence. This model, the oldest and first British motorcycle, went into The Motor Museum, founded by Edmund Dangerfield in London in 1912. When the museum did not re-open after the First World War, the motorcycle came as a gift from Holden himself to this Museum.

This machine represents the birth of the great British motor-cycle industry, once the largest in the world. Most of the early manufacturers were existing bicycle firms that started producing motorcycles. BSA, for example, was Birmingham Small Arms, which originally produced rifles and guns, then bicycles, and then motorcycles.

Colonel Holden demonstrated that motorcycles built on bicycle principles were possible. From this beginning, motorcycles rapidly evolved into something very much built for speed.

THE
BAIRD
"TELEVISOR"

The birth of television

John Logie Baird (1888–1946) has a number of television firsts to his name: the first working television system; the first outside broadcast; the first large-screen television; the first transmission across the Atlantic; the first transmission of colour television; and the first home television system. Baird, who came from Helensburgh, near Glasgow, first demonstrated a mechanical scanning disc system to send and receive images in January 1926. The key was synchronising the process so that the picture could be accurately reconstructed. This is where Baird enjoyed success as a pioneer.

His invention was made from salvaged material – bits of candle wax, lenses from bicycle lamps, lengths of string. Baird's greatest difficulty was obtaining the electronics. In 1929 the company he founded launched a television system for the home, which he called a Televisor. This was the first television you could buy, although not quite the television set we know today. The Televisor received signals broadcast from two BBC radio stations after the radio had gone off air each evening. Owners then had to use two radios to tune in; one for the picture reception and one for the sound. Baird sold a purpose-built dual tuner to go alongside the Televisor. Very few of these were sold and even fewer have survived.

Even though Baird estimated that only around 30 people had a set to receive these first experimental television broadcasts, by 1932 the company had sold a thousand receivers.

The picture appeared as a series of 30 lines, scanned from top to bottom instead of across the screen as in later televisions. The large metal disc inside, spun by a motor in front of a neon lamp, had holes punched in it for projecting the lines. The screen was not much bigger than a pack of cards.

Baird's name remains linked to the experimental days of electro-mechanical systems such as the Televisor, but he was also at the forefront of the development of electronic television in his later work, cementing his position as a true television pioneer.

John Logie Baird (above) in 1928, and a Baird Televisor mechanical television (opposite), 1930.

Bionic hand

Using an i-Limb, 2012 (above), and (opposite) the i-Limb prosthetic hand above the hand of the EMAS arm.

The i-Limb was the first commercially available prosthetic hand to have five individually powered digits: four fingers and a thumb. It had a much more naturalistic range of motion and many more gesture options than earlier prosthetic hands. Its pioneering story is set in Edinburgh.

The city has been at the forefront of prosthetic arm research and development since the early 1960s, when a service was set up to provide limbs for children born with severe birth defects caused by the drug thalidomide, which had been given to pregnant women with disastrous consequences.

This engineering development led eventually to EMAS, the Edinburgh Modular Arm System, the world's first bionic arm, with a powered shoulder, elbow, wrist and hand. A one-off, in 1998 it was fitted to Campbell Aird, a hotelier, whose entire arm had been amputated due to cancer, but who was determined this would not stop his life and work. He was the trial patient, and although it required a lot of maintenance the arm worked for 18 months.

The EMAS arm project was spun off from the National Health Service in 2003 as a company called Touch EMAS, now Touch Bionics, and Campbell Aird's arm has had many thousands of descendants, particularly in the form of the i-Limb. This bionic hand's development has been characterised by a modular approach. If one finger needs servicing it can be easily swapped out. Similarly, if a patient has lost digits but still has the palm of the hand, motorised prosthetic fingers alone may be fitted.

The hands are powered electrically by a battery pack, often in the forearm socket; and they usually run off two sensors which sit on the skin and detect electricity in the muscles. There is thoughtful programming that lets the user choose different grip patterns of the hand: full hand to grab something like a mug, or finger and thumb for a pen. It even has a special setting for working a computer mouse; and the owner can change grips using a smartphone.

The developments in this technology are easy to see; the benefits are life-enhancing.

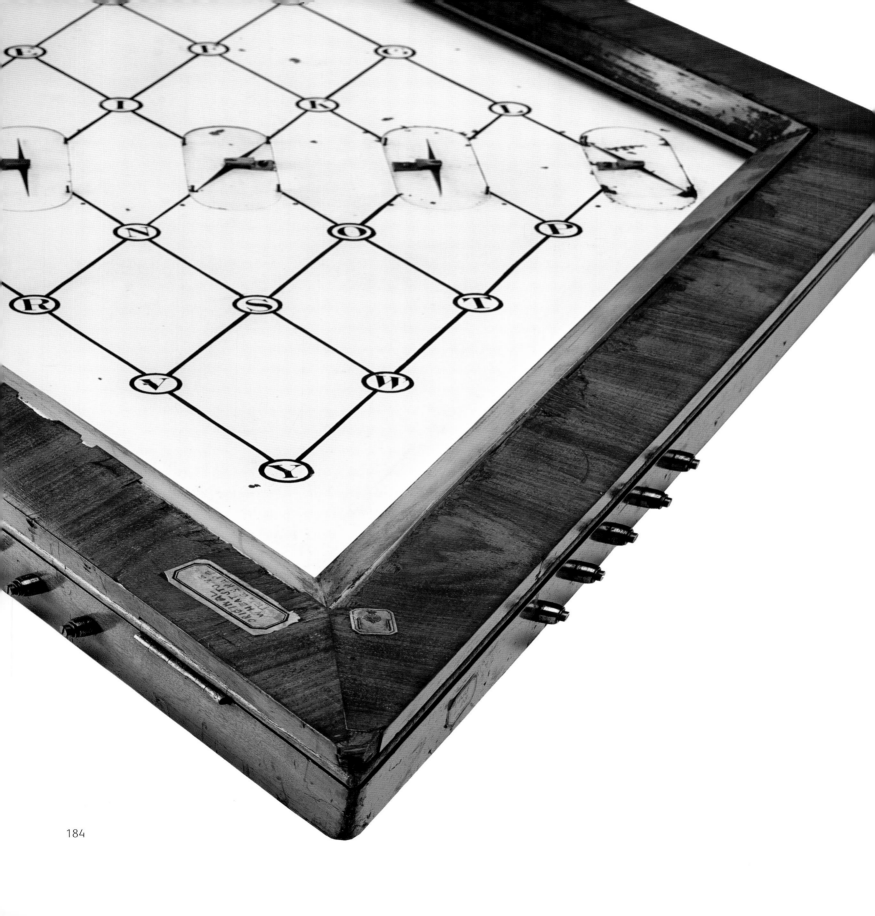

Making connections

During the 1830s the British railway network was expanding rapidly, but companies had no means of communicating down the line. Is it safe for a train to leave the station? Is the train on time? Is there an emergency ahead?

There was no such connection until businessman William Fothergill Cooke (1806–79) and scientist Charles Wheatstone (1802–75) met in 1837. The partnership used inventor Michael Faraday's recent discovery of electro-magnetism to create telegraph communication. On 25 July of that year they sent their first telegraph message.

The pair had invented the diamond-shaped instrument shown here – over 66 centimetres across, with five needles along the centre, set in a mahogany case. By sending currents along a wire, the needles were deflected to point at letters on the grid. This was a system that required two operators: one to look at the dials and read off one letter at a time, another to write down the message. The grid only displayed 20 letters – which was all that could be managed with five needles.

Cooke and Wheatstone demonstrated their five-needle telegraph to the London & Birmingham Railway, with one instrument at each end of a one-and-a-half mile stretch, between Euston and Camden in north London. The network of wires to connect the instruments was embedded in a wooden conduit and laid alongside the railway tracks. However, the five-needle equipment proved complex and impracticable for more than short distances. This motivated the inventors to simplify their system.

A similar method was developed using four, then two, needles. By 1841 Cooke and Wheatstone and others, such as Scottish inventor Alexander Bain and, most importantly, the American Samuel Morse, had invented various code-based single-needle instruments. This quicker system of tapping out a sound or a dot-and-dash based code to spell out the letters succeeded, although the operator had to learn the code.

The impact of electricity on communication – whether telegram, telephone, fax or the World Wide Web – all began with Cooke and Wheatstone's five-needle telegraph. The design of this pioneering communication instrument anticipates beautifully today's keyboard and screen-based computers.

A five-needle telegraph by Cooke and Wheatstone, 1837.

CERN giant

This copper accelerating cavity was the 'go-faster' bit of the particle accelerator known as the Large Electron-Positron Collider, or LEP. The Museum holds one of these substantial pieces of equipment, which came from CERN, the European Organization for Nuclear Research. Based in Geneva, it is the world's largest particle physics laboratory.

As the name implies, LEP accelerated particles, in this case electrons and positrons, and then collided them into each other. Electrons went one way round a 27-kilometre underground tunnel; positrons (which are anti-matter electrons) went the other way round the ring. Many other technologies such as X-ray tubes, and even neon lights, accelerate electrons; LEP was far bigger. The accelerating cavities, of which there were 128, accelerated electrons and positrons by using electromagnetic fields. At four points around the circuit the two beams travelling at nearly the speed of light met head on, the collisions releasing vast amounts of energy.

Inside each two-tonne accelerating cavity is polished copper that is precisely milled, while the outside was left with tool marks. Eleven years of research conducted using LEP led to considerable advances in the understanding of the fundamental building blocks of matter. LEP has been succeeded by the Large Hadron Collider, which has taken the technology another stage forward.

To conduct the experiments at CERN, many innovations were required which impact on our lives, as well as being important for modern scientists. For example, improvements in superconductivity have been important in medical imaging such as MRI scans; and advanced vacuum technology makes solar heat collectors more efficient.

Scientists working with the LEP searched for the Higgs Boson, predicted in 1964 by Peter Higgs of the University of Edinburgh; its existence was eventually proven by experiments using the LEP's successor in the same tunnel, the Large Hadron Collider. The Nobel Prize for physics was awarded jointly to Peter Higgs and François Englert in 2013 following this discovery.

The mouse in the coil

The MRI – Magnetic Resonance Imaging – story highlights the work to develop a laboratory science into a clinically useful technique. Here, as with many other success stories, researchers saw that this could be a great boon to humans and resolved to make it so.

The technique usually shows the location of hydrogen atoms inside an object, and gives an indication of the chemical environment that the hydrogen atoms are in, rendered in three-dimensional pixels. Hydrogen atoms which are part of water molecules in blood will show up differently from hydrogen atoms that are part of fat molecules. MRI can reveal differences within soft tissue that X-rays used in CT (computerised tomography) scans and ultrasound are less sensitive to.

This particular story concerns the University of Aberdeen's contribution to the development of MRI. When Professor John Mallard's research group began work on the technique in 1973, MRI was a theoretical concept. Mallard's group were aware that it could become a highly valuable medical technique.

Their first big success, from 1974, was constructing an apparatus that could scan a mouse, which was a small box with a hole the right size to put a mouse through, and magnetic coils. Although an unsophisticated-looking device, it captured the first MRI image to show injury or illness. The team were hoping for a picture of a mouse; but it showed more than this – that the mouse had a swelling around a broken neck.

The apparatus is in two parts; it would have been inside a much larger magnet to provide a high strength, uniform magnetic field. Magnets, including high power super-conducting magnets, are a vital part of this imaging process. The box has a radio frequency coil, wrapped around a Perspex tube which held the mouse. The outer cylindrical portion has further magnetic coils to produce a variable magnetic field. This apparatus was experimental, and was never intended to survive, which explains the liberal use of masking tape in its construction and repair.

The team went on to create the first clinically useful human image, taken in 1980. The patient was known to have a number of cancers and this image revealed them all, along with another one. Since then, MRI scanning has become one of the great medical diagnostic success stories.

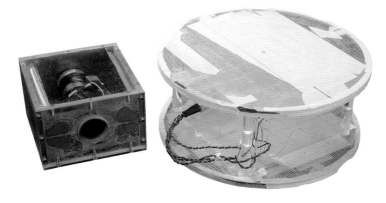

Life-saving discoveries

Sir James Black (1924–2010) presented his many awards for scientific achievement to this Museum, requesting that they be used to inspire young people. By telling his story through the awards he had received, he hoped that others would benefit from science and education as he had.

Black's first achievement was the invention of a successful beta-blocker for use in treating certain types of heart disease. Pre-eminent among the awards was the Nobel Prize for Medicine, awarded in 1988 for his 'discoveries of important principles for drug treatment', and gold medals from the Royal Societies of both London and Edinburgh.

James Black came from a coal-mining family. As a teenager in Fife, his father sent him down the mines for two weeks in the summer holidays as a warning that if he did not study that would be his life. He was only 15 when he won a scholarship to the University of St Andrews.

Specialising in medicine and pharmacology, after a university career he started work for ICI Pharmaceuticals in 1958. He was particularly interested in the problem of how the heart reacts to stress, and the properties of the hormone adrenaline. For someone with a faulty heart, the racing heart from the 'fight or flight' syndrome associated with adrenaline can be dangerous. Using the theory that there must be chemical receptors for adrenaline, Black experimented with molecules which are chemically similar to it to find one which blocked those receptors. Then when the adrenaline is released, the heart would carry on as normal.

Black's great invention from this insight was propranolol, a beta-blocker drug which first came onto the market in 1964. For many years it was an extremely valuable drug for heart patients and also used for relieving symptoms of anxiety. Leaving ICI for Smith, Kline & French, Black developed cimetidine, the first modern drug for stomach ulcers – again a world-leading product.

James Black was knighted in 1981 and admitted to the Order of Merit in 2000. The Nobel Prize marked a lifetime of significant contributions to clinical medicine and pharmacology in the 20th century.

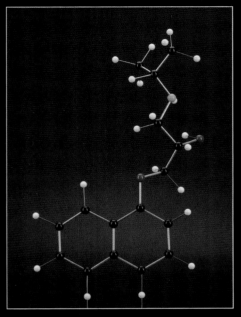

Molecular model for propranolol (above); Sir James Black with the Nobel medal awarded in 1988 (above, right). Medals (below, left to right) awarded to Sir James Black: Junior Anatomy, University of St Andrews, 1942; Mullard medal, Royal Society, London, 1978; Gold medal of the Royal Society of Medicine, 1988–89; Hanbury medal, Royal Pharmaceutical Society of Great Britain, 1991; Gold medal, Royal Society of Edinburgh, 2001; Gold medal, Royal Society of London, 2004; Bronze medal, Royal Philosophical Society of Glasgow, 2002.

Image maker

The centenary of the invention of photography was approaching in the 1930s when the Museum received a substantial gift – a share in the array of early cameras and equipment that had belonged to photography pioneer, William Henry Fox Talbot (1800–77) of Lacock, Wiltshire, England. Talbot's granddaughter Matilda, who inherited the Lacock Abbey estate, wanted to memorialise her happy childhood spent in Dumfriesshire, south-west Scotland, by giving part of the family collection to Scotland's national museum.

A gentleman of considerable means and leisure, Talbot had begun experimenting in the early 1830s with ways of fixing images from a camera obscura; by 1835 he had succeeded in capturing images on silver chloride paper. This was a private hobby and interest, but in 1839 Louis Daguerre in Paris announced his invention of a single positive photographic image on a plate, the daguerreotype. This prompted Talbot to publicise his own discovery, which he called photogenic drawing. He enlisted the help of the astronomer Sir John Herschel – who is credited with coining the word 'photography' – and in 1841 Talbot invented the calotype process.

This was the first photographic process that produced negatives, from which many positive prints could be made. The calotype negative was made by projecting an image through a lens onto chemically sensitised paper inside the camera, on which it formed a latent image. When developed and chemically fixed, this produced a negative image. In turn, this negative was placed in the printing frame with a second piece of sensitised paper beneath it and exposed to sunlight, producing a positive image, which also had to be fixed with chemicals. Talbot used his balance for weighing chemicals, and a domestic iron to apply wax to his negatives, making them more transparent and reducing the printing time.

Matilda Talbot's gift included the quite rudimentary early calotype equipment, a number of calotype images and some other material. There was even a developing box, made on the Lacock estate. Talbot could afford the best, including daguerreotype equipment, sophisticated cameras and lenses, expensive plates and chemicals from Paris.

Talbot's innovations continued with the publication in 1844 of the first book with photographic illustrations, and in the 1850s he developed techniques of etching photographs on metal, contributing to efforts to print photographs alongside typescript.

Carte-de-visite of seated William Henry Fox Talbot holding the lens of a camera, by John Moffat, Edinburgh, 1864.

Appliances of science

The eminent Enlightenment chemist Professor Joseph Black (1728–99) worked and taught at the Universities of Glasgow and Edinburgh. He pioneered quantitative chemical experiments and discovered carbon dioxide. He was also an influential teacher. Against the odds, some of his own laboratory equipment has survived. These examples were used by Black in his lectures in Edinburgh from the mid-1760s onwards.

The equipment comprises laboratory glassware and also his measuring balance. The glassware was made locally, from green bottle glass, in the Leith glassworks just outside Edinburgh. The industry had been founded on the need for wine bottles to hold imported claret; Geddes' glassworks chose to diversify, and advertised that it also made scientific glassware. Archibald Geddes had attended Black's lectures in 1778–80, and Black subsequently invested in his business. It made articles including glass apparatus for impregnating water with 'fixed air', Black's term for carbon dioxide. This made possible the domestic production of 'spa water', so the apparatus was also commercially successful.

Items like this retort (left) and alembic (far right) – names given to these shapes of chemical glassware – were large and relatively crude, but this equipment was used more for demonstrations to large numbers of students than for experimental science. Black also put his research efforts into practical areas, taking a keen interest in the rapidly developing chemical industries in Scotland. Black's own stores were uncovered in an archaeological dig of the University of Edinburgh quadrangle in 2010–11. Included in the finds were toxic substances such as mercury, arsenic and cobalt, together with glass tubes and other vessels, thermometers, and ceramic distillation apparatus made by Josiah Wedgwood, whose sons Black had taught.

When Black was professor, Edinburgh was standing on an intellectual pinnacle. The University had a number of outstanding teachers and many of the thinkers of the Scottish Enlightenment lived in the city. Black himself knew other great contemporary figures from elsewhere, including James Watt, Joseph Priestley and Josiah Wedgwood. The founding Director of this Museum, George Wilson, and Lyon Playfair, one of Black's successors as Professor of Chemistry at the University, showed great foresight when they preserved this equipment, found in a cupboard in 1858. The glassware is a testament to that great age.

High voltage

On 30 April 1930 the very first section of the National Grid was opened with a connection from Portobello Power Station, a few miles east of the centre of Edinburgh. The first electricity pylon in the United Kingdom was built in Scotland, in Bonnyfield near Falkirk in 1928, and over the next few years the landscape was rapidly changed by a network of pylons and cables. There was considerable excitement about the development and the opportunities that electricity as a public utility might bring.

The development of the National Grid was one of the most profound technological changes of the 20th century, transforming everyday lives and industry. Prior to the Grid, power stations were more local, with little regulation, and connections were often unreliable. By 1935, seven grid areas had been created and commercial operation across the United Kingdom began.

The Grid continued to evolve and expand. In the 1940s and 1950s large scale hydroelectric schemes were established across the north of Scotland. By the 1960s, 90 per cent of people living in the Highlands were connected; for the first time they were able to install life-changing electrical appliances such as cookers and refrigerators, and operate electric farm machinery, without a stand-alone generator.

It is important for the Museum to explore the history of how electricity gets from where it is generated to where it is needed, and to relate that to the renewable energy technologies of today which might be further away from industrial centres.

This isolator was used at the substation which connected Portobello Power Station to the National Grid. Although parts of the substation were replaced over time, this section dates from the opening of the National Grid in 1930. It is part of five pieces of high voltage transmission equipment collected by the Museum shortly after the closure of the substation in 1989. At almost 3 metres high, the isolator was used to disconnect the electrical circuit, making it safe for engineers to repair and maintain other pieces of equipment.

A model museum

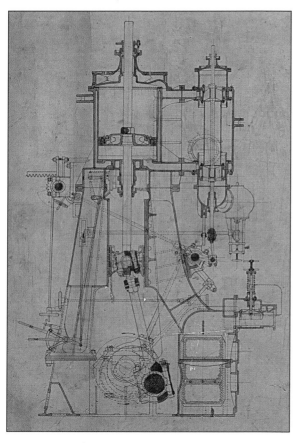

A plan of the *Zealandia* engine, by Elder & Co., Glasgow.

During the late 19th and early 20th century, the Museum's work-shop produced some of the most advanced, complex and clever engineering models in the world. These models are still in the Museum's collection.

In the 1860s, the workshop began building models of the most advanced technologies of the time. So many innovations – such as steam engines, civil-engineering projects and lighthouses – were too big to be acquired, so models were built to scale.

The intricate example featured here is a marine engine of a type made for two ships, *Zealandia* and *Australia*, both launched in 1875. The Museum obtained the engine drawings at the same time as the full-scale version was being built in the Clyde shipyards of Glasgow by Elder & Co. It took four years to build the model and close inspection of the result shows why. It was labour-intensive work, with the model-makers employing materials and engineering techniques very close to the original, such as miniature riveting.

Early models, like an 1880s Foster stereo printing press based on one used by the *Scotsman* newspaper, were not powered by electricity: a staff member in the gallery turned a handle to animate them. With the advent of electricity, however, push-button models were introduced. Many people in Scotland remember coming to the Museum as children and pressing the buttons of these models on display.

Full-size steam engines, dating to the late 19th century, are also exhibited alongside the intricate scale models.

The Museum's workshop closed in the 1970s. The machinery, lathes and machine tools were saved, and conservators use them still for restoration work to the models – in this way a strong connection with the model-makers of the past continues.

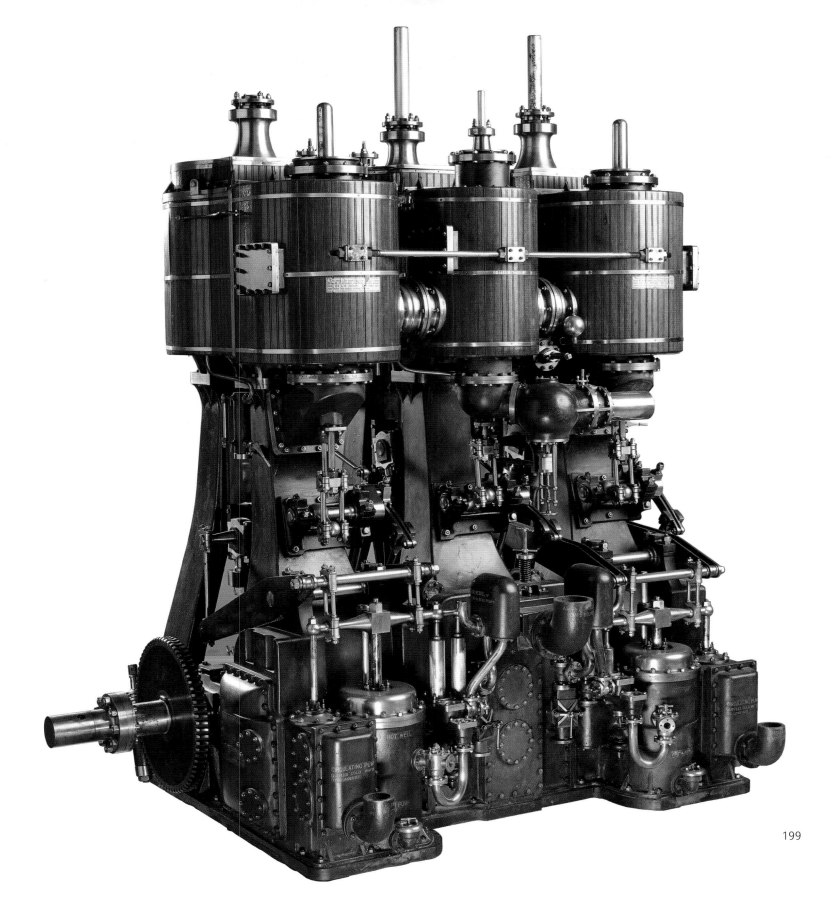

World Cultures

The World Cultures collections are the largest in Scotland and internationally important. They incorporate decorative arts, fine arts, ethnographic and archaeological collections from all the cultures beyond Europe and those of the ancient world. Their history speaks to the origins of the Museum, with internationalism and national benefit as core ideals. They are extraordinarily diverse, with the oldest piece an Egyptian Paleolithic hand axe at 40,000 years old, and one of the newest acquisitions *Casualty of War: A Portrait of Maharaja Duleep Singh* (2013) by the British Sikh artists The Singh Twins.

These collections are the result of a merger of a number of early and important collections, including that of the University of Edinburgh (transferred in the 1850s), and the National Museum of Antiquities of Scotland (transferred in the 1950s). The collections from Oceania, Africa and North America are connected to early voyages of exploration and trade as well as government. They can be traced to figures such as Captain James Cook (1728–79) and Sir Thomas Makdougall Brisbane (1773–1860). Scots working for the Hudson's Bay Company in Canada in the mid-19th century, such as Dr John Rae (1813–93), gifted an exceptional collection of Dene and Inuit material. In the 19th and early 20th century, missionaries were significant contributors to the Africa and Oceania collections, including most notably David Livingstone (1813–73).

From the mid-19th century the Museum set about collecting decorative and industrial arts from Asia and the Middle East. Scots in the civil and military service of the East India Company contributed to the building of the collections from South Asia. Especially noteworthy are the Iranian collections, formed under the directorship of Sir Robert Murdoch Smith. Significant areas for East Asia are the Chinese inscribed oracle bones, the lacquer wares and more recent propaganda arts from the People's Republic of China, as well as Japanese 19th-century woodblock prints, early modern ceramics and Korean ceramics.

Within the Ancient Mediterranean collection there is a strikingly high proportion of pieces which have a direct association with pioneers in archaeology, most notably the Scot Alexander Henry Rhind (1833–63) and Sir William Matthew Flinders Petrie FRS (1853–1942). Much of the collection is of outstanding artistic merit due to the eye and scholarship of Cyril Aldred who shaped the collection during his long tenure as expert Egyptologist from 1937 to 1974.

Since its founding, the Museum has collected the contemporary on a global scale which remains a tradition today. Curators work with artists, communities and scholars to reframe historical relationships and provide new interpretations of our collections aiming to broaden participation and inspire the widest possible audiences.

The Qurna queen

The Second Intermediate Period (*c.*1750–1550 BC) was a time of civil war and foreign occupation in ancient Egypt. This burial offers rich insights into the funerary practices, craft production and trade during this less well known period of Egyptian history.

The coffin is painted in blue and yellow, highlighted with extensive gilding. It is decorated with a design typical of the period, known as *rishi* style (Arabic for 'feathered'), with the wings of a vulture goddess enfolding the lid to protect the body. Based on analysis of the remains, the coffin belonged to a young woman, probably in her early twenties. It is a strikingly beautiful object, intended to ensure her eternal life. Her identity is a mystery, as her name and titles on the coffin lid are damaged, but evidence suggests that she was a member of the royal family. This coffin was found as part of a larger group of objects, making it the only intact royal burial outside Egypt.

At the time, the north of Egypt was occupied by people from western Asia called the Hyksos, while the pharaohs of the 17th Dynasty ruled southern Egypt from Thebes (modern Luxor). Although the power and wealth of these pharaohs were diminished, the burial still contained over a hundred objects, including many precious items from other regions. For instance, incredibly thin-walled and beautifully burnished Kerma beakers found amongst them were imports or gifts from Nubia (modern Sudan).

Unfortunately, poorly executed mummification meant that the coffin contained just skeletal remains. A child was found buried alongside in a plain rectangular coffin. Both woman and child had matching sets of jewellery, including some of the earliest attested examples of earrings discovered in Egypt and a beautiful crafted necklace of over 1600 gold annular beads. Scientific analysis conducted by the Museum in 2008 revealed the earrings to be 95 per cent pure gold.

The burial was excavated in 1908 at Sheikh Abd el-Qurna, on the west bank at Thebes, by Sir William Matthew Flinders Petrie (1853–1942), often called the 'Father of Egyptian Archaeology'. Petrie's systematic excavation and recording means we know the precise arrangement of the objects within the burial as it was originally found. Petrie wanted to ensure that objects stayed together and would be kept secure: at the time, this was the largest group of goldwork to have left Egypt. Curator Edwin Ward (1880–1934), a future director of this Museum, had excavated in Egypt with Petrie – so this valuable burial group came to Scotland.

The Qurna burial as found by Sir William Matthew Flinders Petrie at Sheikh Abd el-Qurna, Thebes, Egypt, 1908.

Tomb hunter

Portrait of Alexander Henry Rhind by Alexander S Mackay, oil on canvas, 1874.

The Scot Alexander Henry Rhind (1833–63) was the first experienced archaeologist to work in Egypt. Today Sir William Matthew Flinders Petrie is renowned as the 'Father of Egyptian Archaeology', but Rhind was systematically recording detailed plans and preserving even the simplest artefacts, first in Scotland and then Egypt, almost 30 years before Petrie.

Dismayed at the widespread looting and unsystematic digging in Egypt, Rhind set himself the task of locating an intact tomb. If he could determine the exact contents and arrangement of objects within a burial, he could better understand Egyptian funerary practices and how they changed over time.

Excavating on the west bank of Thebes, Egypt, Rhind found just such a tomb. It had been re-used from an earlier period, but the lower chambers were sealed and untouched. Inside was a family tomb with the burials of ten individuals, added over time. In the entrance corridor stood the extraordinary 2-metre long funerary canopy featured here, a unique artefact, which may have been used to transport a mummy to the tomb. It combines the forms of a coffin with a vaulted roof representing the sky and an ancient Egyptian temple in miniature. The façade has a frieze of protective cobras along the top supported by papyrus-shaped columns, and a doorway with an open lintel to allow the passage of the sun. The decoration is painted in stunning reds, blues and yellows. The top is painted with a pattern reminiscent of a bead-net shroud: a net of faience beads placed over a mummy as a protective device.

The canopy is inscribed for Montsuef, a local high official. A funerary papyrus found with his mummy dates his burial to precisely 9 BC. Montsuef's life and career spanned the reign of Cleopatra VII, the last queen of Egypt, and Egypt's conquest by the Roman Emperor Augustus. The entire burial group discovered by Rhind, recorded in great detail and brought to Edinburgh, provides a fascinating snapshot of an important Egyptian family living under foreign rule. The burial items preserved many ancient Egyptian traditions, while also incorporating Graeco-Roman influences.

Rhind's travel to Egypt's warm, dry climate was partially motivated by his ill-health, but he died of tuberculosis just one month shy of his 30th birthday. The contributions that he made to both Egyptian and Scottish archaeology were remarkable for someone so young. One can only imagine what he might have achieved had he lived longer.

A weighty ruler

This carved stone panel from the palace of Ashurnasirpal II (883–59 BC), King of the Assyrian Empire, shows one of the most powerful rulers in ancient history. It was one of many panels that lined the walls in the palace in ancient Kalhu (now Nimrud in modern Iraq), intended to create a sense of awe. Key in expanding the Assyrian Empire, Ashurnasirpal II led 14 military campaigns against the Aramaeans, Syro-Hittites and others.

Ancient Assyrian kings were expected to be conquerors and their power was defined by their ability to defend and enlarge their territory. As such, Ashurnasirpal II was often presented as blood-thirsty and merciless. The cuneiform inscription on this relief describes him as 'fearless in battle, a mighty flood-tide which has no opponent', but also as a 'marvellous shepherd'.

The relief shows the king crowned and wearing elaborate robes. It is on a grand scale, just larger than life-size at 2.4 metres high and 2.2 metres wide. Up close there are minute details, rosettes and tiny figures of deities embroidered on the king's robes. He holds an offering cup to the gods, while an attendant with a fly-whisk and a cloth faces him. Originally the panel would have been colourfully painted; traces of red can still be seen on the robes.

The inscription runs along the bottom, a standard text about the king's divine favour, conquests and the founding of his new capital at Kalhu – but on this relief the scribe seems to have lost his place and copied a section twice. Running out of space at the bottom, the script trickles over the border of the king's robes. The panel may be imposing, but this gives it a human element.

The palace of Ashurnasirpal II was excavated in the 1840s by the English archaeologist Sir Austen Henry Layard (1817–94). This relief belonged to Sir James Young Simpson (1811–70), the pioneering Edinburgh doctor who in 1847 discovered the use of chloroform as an anaesthetic. He gave it to the Society of Antiquaries of Scotland in 1865 and hence to the Museum.

At over 2 tonnes in weight, moving the mighty panel to its current position in the Museum, even with the assistance of modern technology, took Herculean efforts.

Sir James Young Simpson, from an album of early photographs compiled by Dr John Adamson, c.1860s.

The Edinburgh painter

The city of Edinburgh has its own named Athenian Greek vase artist – the 'Edinburgh Painter'.

Sir John Beazley (1885–1970), Professor of Classical Archaeology at Oxford, developed identifications of specific artists' hands responsible for the decoration of ancient Athenian Greek vases. Beazley bestowed the name on the artist who was responsible for the decoration of two vases in the Museum's collection in Edinburgh. Otherwise the artist is anonymous.

One of the two vases was found in Italy, where many vessels decorated by the Edinburgh Painter have been found, brought there from Athens. Coastal Italy and Sicily were so densely inhabited by Greek settlers that the area later became known as Magna Graecia, 'Great Greece'. This vase probably came from a burial, since it is a *lekythos* or oil vase. These were used to anoint the dead and are frequently found in tombs.

The Edinburgh Painter specialised in *lekythoi* and was active around 500 BC. At the time, the typical painting style was 'black-figure', featuring figures painted in black on vessels' plain red-clay background. However, the Edinburgh Painter used an innovative variation in which a white background was added, a process that was probably both expensive and fragile. He was among the earliest practitioners of this technique.

This vase features a scene from the *Iliad*, one that would be appropriate for a burial context. It is a rare pictorial representation of the climax in Homer's epic poem about the war between the Greeks and the Trojans. After the Greek hero Achilles killed Hector, Prince of Troy, he dragged Hector's body behind his chariot around the city of Troy, dishonouring the body in angry vengeance. Finally, King Priam begged Achilles for the return of the body of his son, pleading with him to think of his own dear father. The Greek hero relented, moved by his enemy's poignant plea. This vase adds a visual dimension to our understanding of the epic, and how the ancient Greeks would have related to these stories in their own lives. This scene on a funerary vase might have prompted mourners to reflect on the poem's message about the universality of grief. The Edinburgh Painter's work is a way of understanding personal loss through poetry, translated into visual form.

Riding the whale

Woodblock prints were a part of everyday life in Japan during the Edo period (1615–1868). Ephemeral and affordable, they were like posters and magazines today. A single sheet print was equivalent in price to a double helping of noodles.

At that time Japan was a nation at peace, and had been so since about 1615 when a century of civil wars was brought to an end. Prints like this were not meant to be representations of contemporary life, but fantastical, idealistic visions of the past. Hollywood movies today similarly present us with the strong warrior hero out to save the world.

Warriors from the past swashbuckle in these visual prints. This example by Utagawa Kuniyoshi (1797–1861) shows a semi-legendary warrior of the early 17th century, carrying out a feat of superhuman strength. Leaping onto the back of a whale which is threatening people's lives, he plunges his sword into the animal, deep enough to kill it. It is a fantastically dynamic composition, with the huge whale in dramatic black and white tones set against the roiling blue waves. Almost the entire composition is taken up by the body of the whale – with, if you look carefully, the tiny figure of the renowned warrior Miyamoto Musashi riding upon its back.

The ruling military élite in Japan carried out periodic strict crack-downs to enforce censorship regulations; this did not allow representation of contemporary events, as that was seen to be potentially disruptive. Change came after the full opening of Japan with the Meiji Restoration of 1868. From then, many Japanese people were more interested in what was unfamiliar to them, such as Western costume, buildings, steam trains and steamships. Western collectors in turn sought traditional imagery and representations of Japanese scenes unfamiliar to them.

As a result, high-quality visual material was imported into Europe in large quantities in the 1880s. The *japonisme* boom inspired artists – Van Gogh and Monet among others – who admired the unique aesthetic qualities of these woodblock prints. The desire to have a representative collection of cultures, peoples and art forms from countries across the world, Japan among them, was key to the early collecting activities of this Museum. There are now more than 4000 Japanese prints in the Museum's collection.

Tea ceremony

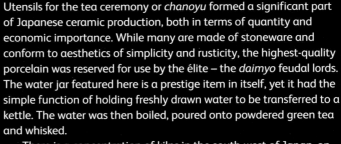

Utensils for the tea ceremony or *chanoyu* formed a significant part of Japanese ceramic production, both in terms of quantity and economic importance. While many are made of stoneware and conform to aesthetics of simplicity and rusticity, the highest-quality porcelain was reserved for use by the élite – the *daimyo* feudal lords. The water jar featured here is a prestige item in itself, yet it had the simple function of holding freshly drawn water to be transferred to a kettle. The water was then boiled, poured onto powdered green tea and whisked.

There is a concentration of kilns in the south-west of Japan, on the island of Kyushu. This jar was made, probably in the early 19th century, at Hirado Mikawachi, which specialised in pure white, high-quality porcelain with underglaze cobalt blue decoration and often with sculpted elements. This piece portrays a lively thrashing fish, a carp, as the moulded finial to lift the lid. The body of the jar features painted carp and lion-dogs (a kind of mythological beast). These energetic creatures spring and weave their way through water, reflecting the purpose of the jar.

The jar has a beautiful spherical form, the lid continuing the line of the curve of the body. The finial on top has very delicate open-work frills representing the water spraying around the fish; these, perhaps inevitably, have become broken over time, and have been repaired in a traditional technique called *kintsugi* (literally, 'gold join'), using lacquer as adhesive, mixed with gold powder. The careful repair openly acknowledges the damage suffered, but also testifies to how much the work is valued.

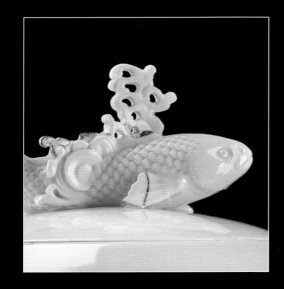

The water jar is part of a substantial donation of Japanese and Chinese ceramics given to the Museum by David and Anne Hyatt King in 2015, thanks to support from the Art Fund. David Hyatt King (1946–2016) collected these rare and special pieces from the 1960s. Just a few years ago he travelled to Japan and visited their places of manufacture for the first time. He was very enthused, and indeed moved, by seeing for himself the kilns that made many of the items in his collection – kilns that remain in operation today.

216

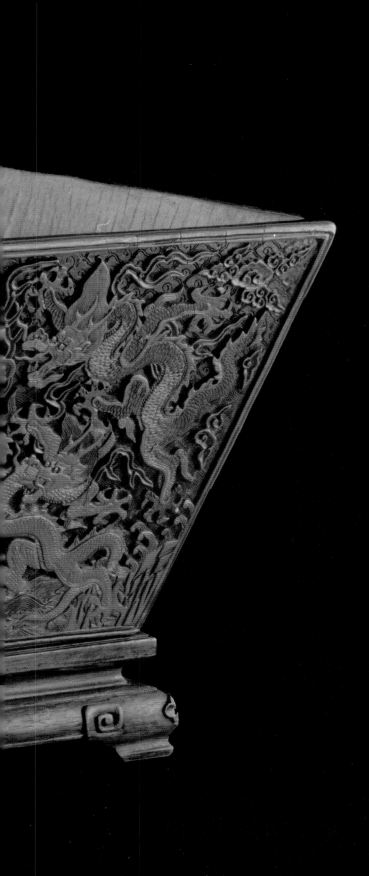

Measure of life

Rice is the agricultural basis of civilisation across East Asia. It is the staff of life: 'Man cannot live by rice alone, but Man cannot live without rice', as the Chinese saying goes.
A measuring vessel for rice represents the ability of people to eat and life to function, so for the Chinese imperial court to use something as seemingly quotidian as a rice measure is deeply symbolic – for rice is wealth, and the very basis of the economy.

This rice measure, at c.32 centimetres square, is a large, ostentatious and rare item that would have attracted attention and sat at the very centre of court rituals. Ritual is important in Chinese civilisation as it gives order to the universe, the world and the workings of society. An elaborate suite of court rituals continued through a long sweep of Chinese history. The rice measure in the Museum's collection played an important role in the performance of such rituals within the imperial court.

The measure is constructed of a wooden core overlaid with multiple layers of lacquer. The material and base colour are highly symbolic. Lacquer is the sap of the tree *Toxicidendron*. Red lacquer, with intricate patterns on each side carved deep into it, is characteristically Chinese. Red is the colour of happiness and prosperity in China, with positive associations. In contrast, Korean lacquer tends to be black with mother-of-pearl inlay, and Japanese lacquer employs plentiful gold. Though red predominates on this piece, the maker has skilfully carved through the layers, creating motifs in green and brown.

There are many symbols carved into the surface: on each side five dragons cavort in clouds above mountains and the sea. Among these, the central dragon holds aloft *lingzhi*, a fungus symbolising immortality, and above is a single Chinese character, either Abundance (*wan*) or Longevity (*shou*).

The supreme quality of workmanship and large scale distinguish this piece, which bears meanings beyond its original purpose.

Seat of power

This large object from China is a grand imperial seat. A throne may be imagined as a unique item, whereas seats like this one were simply designated places where only the Emperor could sit.

The Imperial Palace in China was divided up hierarchically. Protocol became less formal as one progressed into the interior quarters. This seat was probably designed for one of these less formal spaces.

The evidence for this supposition is the display shelves fitted into the piece, where the Emperor kept intriguing or beautiful artefacts near to hand. He could take out and contemplate these trinkets in idle moments, perhaps when no one was addressing him or bringing a petition to his attention. Having these objects around his person allowed the Emperor to display his knowledge and intellectual curiosity about the world.

The seat is made of lacquered wood, using a black lacquer ground with elaborate gold decoration. This draws on the language of auspicious symbolism where animals and plants convey messages of success, good fortune and longevity. Some of the images are based on verbal puns drawing on the high number of homophones in the Chinese language: for example, the word for 'bat' sounds similar to the word for 'happiness', even though the two words are written differently. The decorations are not just random choices.

The Emperor often moved between rooms in a palace, between buildings, even between cities; this imperial seat could be easily dismantled and packed up, then reassembled like flat-pack furniture today. It has an ingenious construction, technically very sophisticated as well as beautiful in its decoration.

There are echoes here in the royal courts of Scotland and England, which used to be peripatetic. Courtiers could take the room decoration with them – literally roll it up, put it in boxes, transport it, hang it up – and a room would look exactly as it did in its previous location. The host, the courtly or lordly household, would foot the bill. The same held true in China.

An imperial 'how-to' guide

Knowing how to behave correctly was at the heart of the Chinese imperial system. Rank played a large role within early modern Chinese society and was reflected clearly in dress and accessories. The Museum's set of 65 folios, *Regulations for Ceremonial Paraphernalia of the Qing Dynasty*, is a luxury 'how to' guide for labyrinthine imperial rituals. There was always a need for instructions on how these rituals should be performed, and the importance and value placed upon them, as well as the rarity of many of the rituals, meant that the guides were beautifully and carefully made, handwritten and illustrated. This complexity could not all be kept in the head.

Codified according to rank, dress was an important part of the Chinese court. Badges and insignia, received as marks of promotion, were proudly worn. The nuances of court etiquette and the social structure were underpinned by official examinations – in itself a large and highly structured system. The system was in theory merit-based, so by taking exams a court official could rise through the ranks.

Regulations for Ceremonial Paraphernalia of the Qing Dynasty consists of exquisite hand-painted images and calligraphy on silk, each piece mounted on stiff *xuan* paper. Divided into six parts, the guide covers multiple aspects of court etiquette: the use of ceremonial vessels of various types, dress, musical instruments, insignia, weaponry and even scientific equipment. It was an illustrated conclusion to the lengthy efforts of the Qianlong Emperor (r.1736–95) to regulate the numerous ritual codes and procedures of his court. As many as 27 court painters and calligraphers worked on the commission.

A conscientious courtier would do his best to get everything absolutely right, because there was bound to be someone overseeing him who would know better, would be more experienced, and would point out if he got it wrong. A mistake in carrying out these rituals might not be fatal, but it was certainly not advantageous for a courtier's career. The guides to the rituals – objects of beauty in themselves – were essential tools.

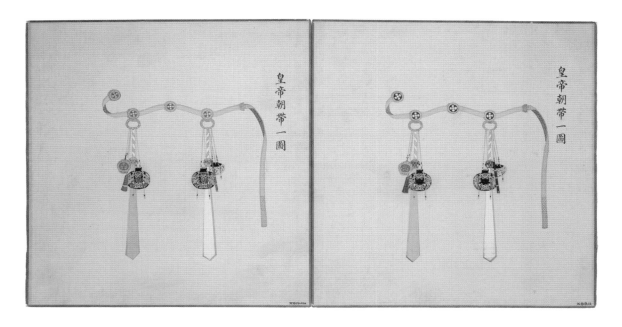

Nature crystallised

Beauty in ceramics comes in various shapes and sizes, and at a diameter of over half a metre, this Chinese fish bowl is beauty on a very large scale.

Porcelain was China's primary export in the 17th to 19th centuries; indeed this is what the term 'china' means in English. Yet of the vast quantities of porcelain produced in China, very little exists as enormous as this bowl. Its production is a highly successful technical achievement, destined for the imperial court.

During the Han Dynasty (206 BCE–220 CE), makers of ceramics in China discovered kaolin, a type of clay suitable for making high-quality porcelain. The sheer weight in a large item often caused it to collapse or distort during the firing process. Because this impeded the production of other goods, a ban was issued on the making of large porcelain pieces in 1571.

The size of this bowl in the Museum's collection required it to be very thickly potted. Even if they were thick enough to withstand firing, many such bowls broke in the extreme cold of winter. As a result, only six large bowls of this type are known to exist, and the Museum has two.

Such bowls were used as fish-ponds to contain what is represented on the outside – attractive red and yellow lotuses with fish swimming among them. The imperial palace was an artificially constructed environment, with garden areas, and a bowl like this could be moved around and set up anywhere inside the building. Made as a decorative item, possibly to hold carp, the illustration on the bowl provides a little crystallisation of nature.

The decorative technique on this bowl is known as *wucai*, or 'five colours', the five elements typically being the white porcelain body, dark cobalt outlines, and red, green and yellow painted enamels. *Wucai* was the most complex of colour palettes used in Chinese ceramic history. It was especially popular from the mid-1500s to early 1600s.

This bowl has a mark on the interior rim indicating the Longqing reign, from 1567 to 1572. As this is precisely around the time of the 1571 ban on giant pieces, this bowl is a rare survival of its type.

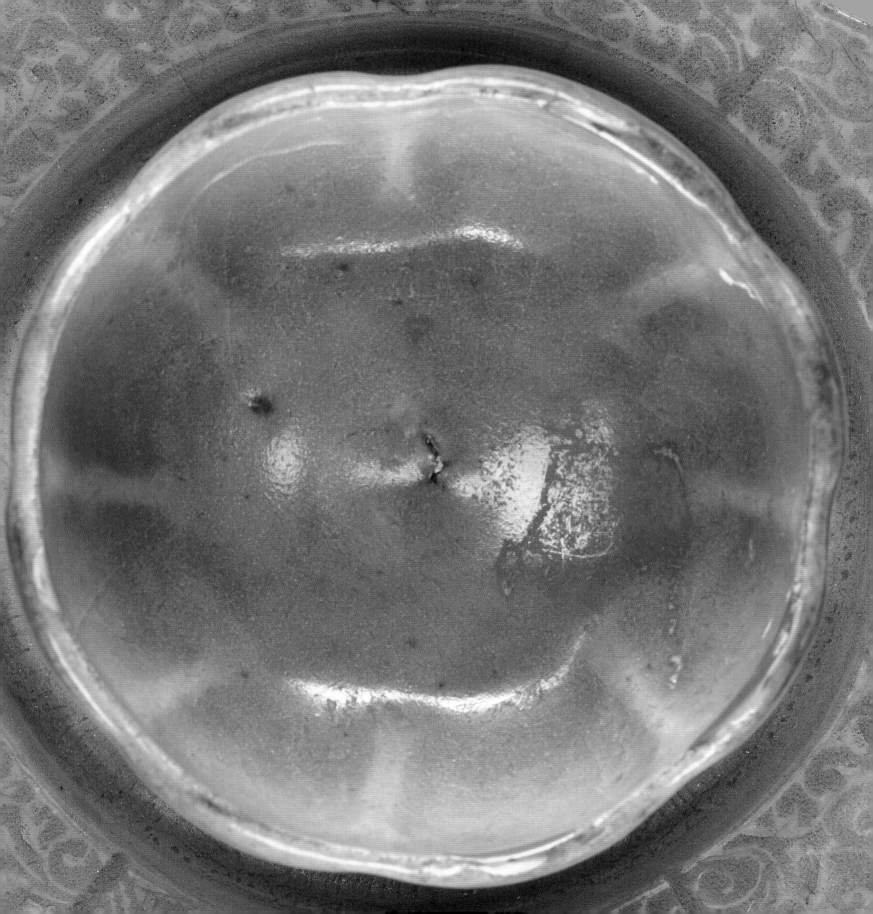

Enlightenment in celadon

The greatest achievement of Korean ceramics is celadon, a rich, sea-green glaze. Celadon stoneware originated in China in the 11th century, but in Korea it was developed in a particular shade of green which is instantly recognisable, even at a distance, as Korean.

This cup and stand are made of stoneware, which is a brown colour – and this can be seen on the unglazed base where some of the technical secrets are revealed. The pieces display the refined technique of underglaze inlay for the decoration of small flowers, lotus petals and scrolling leaf patterns. This involved incising the design into dry clay body, filling it with white slip and then covering with the translucent celadon glaze. The process required repeated firings for all of these effects to emerge. Pieces of this type are always beautifully finished; the workshops generally had such exacting standards that they would destroy those that were substandard, so only good quality pieces survive.

The shape is a well-established, traditional one. A small wine or tea-cup would be given a grander setting with a stand in the form of a lotus. This flower has religious associations – the pure white lotus emerges from the filth and mud of existence and so represents Buddhist enlightenment.

This cup and stand was given to the Museum by Lieutenant-Colonel Kenneth Dingwall DSO (1869–1946), an avid collector of East Asian ceramics and founding member of the Oriental Ceramics Society. There are skilled repairs in gold lacquer on the rims of both parts, suggesting that they were previously in a Japanese collection as this technique was developed in Japan. Many of the Korean ceramics in the Museum's collection came via Japan. Korean ceramics were highly popular there, after the Japanese invasion of the 1590s, when Korean technology and technicians were taken back to Japan. They were a novel and popular form of ceramics that became prestigious and expensive objects in their new home.

New speaks to old

This, the largest Maori vessel in European collections, perhaps of any outside New Zealand, used to sit in the stores of the Museum. It was a mystery object that seemed odd in various ways. Underneath it looked more like a river canoe, but other parts looked like an original Maori war canoe, a *waka taua*, and a rather early one at that. Yet at 6 metres in length it was too short, as war canoes were generally between 20 and 30 metres long, and it had a crude stern (the back or far end of the canoe), which had been added later. A curator recognised its potential importance and wanted to give the *waka* the honour it deserved.

The specialist Roger Neich from Auckland confirmed its authenticity in 2006, dating its carvings to the 1830s or even earlier, from the Bay of Plenty in North Island. It is likely that at some time two different vessels had been put together, with the side strakes (planks forming the sides of the vessel, in this case at the top) from a larger war canoe cut in half and arranged along each side. The stern was an early museum addition.

The *waka* came to the Museum as part of the University of Edinburgh collections; it appears to have been given to the University in 1827, having been in Kelso in the Scottish Borders.

Research linked it to Thomas Makdougall Brisbane (1773–1860), Governor of New South Wales in Australia between 1821 and 1825, after whom Brisbane, Queensland, is named. Whether it was a diplomatic gift or exchanged goods is not known.

Now the *waka* consists of two conjoined parts, the original vessel and a new *taurapa*, the stern with its post, which the Museum commissioned from George Nuku, a notable Maori artist who works in PMMA (Perspex), with abalone insets. The tall stern post shows all the characteristics of Maori war canoes and consists of elaborate open-work carving. Nuku replaced a small figure, usually found at the base facing into the canoe, with a stylised face with slanted eyes and a thistle on the forehead to acknowledge the historical context of the project. In this way, a conservation and restoration project also became an artistic creative process.

Nuku has honoured the master carvers who had worked on the canoe before him: reinterpreting traditional Maori designs, following the traditions of his forefathers and the way they worked, but bringing new materials into the process, new beauty and a 21st-century sensibility.

George Nuku (above) carving the new stern post at the Museum; and (right) a detail of the stern post in situ, showing the thistle that was included by Nuku as a reference to Scotland.

Prestige and power

The Museum is in the fortunate position of possessing a range of objects connected to the pioneering voyages of Captain James Cook (1728–79). Among them are three gorgets or ceremonial collars from Tahiti, one of the Society Islands in French Polynesia.

Drawings and paintings created by the artists who accompanied Cook's voyages depict leading warriors standing on elevated platforms of large double canoes wearing such collars, and we know that they were reserved for chiefly clans and priests. The materials used – shiny sharks' teeth and shimmering dog hair – were highly valued. Gorgets emphasised the prestige and status of their wearers and were considered appropriate tributes and gifts of exchange within hierarchical Tahitian society. That was probably why James Cook and prominent members of his crew were presented with such collars, being considered powerful visitors.

There are about 50 Tahitian gorgets in collections around the world and this example is among the best preserved. All collars were collected in the last quarter of the 18th century, which suggests that manufacture was given up after that point. The complexity and extraordinary materials indicate that the gorgets were the work of skilled artisans. Starting with a frame of aerial roots, coconut fibres were plaited into strings, and these were woven to make a bed for iridescent black birds' feathers to be attached. After that came a band of sharks' teeth, carefully graded in size, with the smaller ones closer to the neck. As only ten to twelve suitable teeth could be taken from a single shark, between seven and 15 sharks would have been killed just to obtain enough teeth for one collar. White dog hair was then added, and finally pearl shell.

Sharks' teeth and dog hair were both associated with ancestral power. A warrior wearing such a collar on his chest and one on his back would have been likened to someone in the mouth of a shark, or even to a shark itself, taking on all its properties and spiritual power.

Captain Cook was stabbed to death in Hawai'i during a violent confrontation with the islanders. This gorget was among items given to his widow. She passed it on to Sir John Pringle (1707–82) who presented it to the Society of Antiquaries of Scotland in 1781 and hence to the Museum.

Sacred bowl

In the Admiralty Islands, in north-eastern Papua New Guinea, the skulls of important ancestors were kept in men's houses, sometimes in large wooden bowls like this one. When a great feast took place, an ancestral skull could be displayed in a bowl suspended outside the house and a leader would present devotional offerings to it. He would have considered the ancestor from which the skull was taken as his guardian spirit. In front of the assembled community he informed the spirit that the feast was given in its honour. There would be dancing and ceremonial exchanges and food was served in wooden bowls – pork, yams, tubers, different festive ceremonial delicacies, with soup poured over them.

Commemorative ritual feasting ensured that rights to land and leadership were transferred in the correct way, that people were honoured and, before Christianity came, that the spirit of the deceased reached its destination safely. Carved wooden bowls were also used in healing rituals to hold liquids with magical or spiritual characteristics, for marriage feasts and in the context of female initiations.

This is a comparatively large bowl at just over a metre across,

and, characteristic of these islands, it is hemispherical and stands on four feet. It is worked from hardwood with fretwork handles attached using a mastic or putty from the parinarium nut.

The decoration includes spirals, and – a rarity – a lizard on each side. The bowl is further ornamented with carved relief patterns on the outer wall, and black and red pigments. Designs such as zig-zags, triangles and arcs also appear on other carved objects from the area and are associated with tattooing and tattoo patterns. The series of disc shapes on the belly derives from an ornament worn on the chest or on the forehead, a clamshell disc with a carved turtle shell disc on top, symbolic of rank and prestige.

John Young Buchanan (1844–1925), a chemist and oceano-grapher, collected the bowl. He sailed on HMS *Challenger*, a voyage of scientific exploration around the world between 1872 and 1876. On that expedition, 243 members set out but only 144 returned, mostly due to desertion. This bowl is one of five that Buchanan purchased; he gave them to the Society of Antiquaries of Scotland in 1901, and three were transferred to this Museum in 1956.

Badge of office

Portrait of a statesman or a warrior? A diplomatic gift or a badge of office? These are some of the questions we can ask of this superlative club handed to James Bruce (1811–63), 8th Earl of Elgin, during his time as Governor General of Canada from 1847 to 1854. Naturalistic in style, masterful in execution, this is one of the most imposing effigy carvings made by the indigenous people of Northeastern North America in the early to mid-19th century, most likely the work of the people known as the Iroquois. The Iroquois, or more properly the Haudenosaunee, Confederacy was one of the most powerful indigenous political alliances in the early colonial period, controlling territories bordering both French and British settlements.

Ball-headed clubs were effective weapons used in early colonial warfare, but by the 18th and 19th century other weapons had superseded them. This club could certainly have served the purposes of war, but most importantly combined symbolic materials with spiritual meanings.

The refined carving shows the widespread indigenous practice of body painting and tattooing and pays particular attention to the hairstyle. The head is shown as mostly shaved, with feathers and red wool added to the hair and held in place by an ornament of tin and iron. Originally the eyes are likely to have been infilled with reflective materials. The club is perfectly balanced and its elongated handle is further notched, painted and decorated with cut feathers at the bottom.

It was most likely a badge of office, a symbol of power and statecraft. The transfer from its original owner to James Bruce was undoubtedly a political and symbolic gesture of some significance. As Governor General at a time of great political turbulence, Bruce met with and was actively petitioned by leaders from a number of indigenous nations. Bruce saw his role as a nation-builder and his term as Governor General marks the acceptance by British colonial authorities of the principle of self-government or 'responsible government' in Canada. Bruce acknowledged the authority of the Canadian Parliament, a shift that led to Canadian Confederation in 1867.

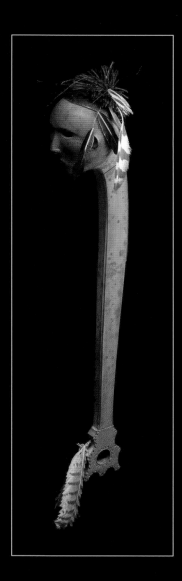

Model *munka*

Like many 19th-century donors, when Dr John Rae (1813–93) recorded the provenance of this model canoe, he handed the Museum a puzzle that has prompted a long discussion. Three model canoes were gifted posthumously to the University of Edinburgh, said to be from Vancouver Island, Canada. This canoe was identified as a war canoe and linked to the Kwakwaka'wakw people.

This is a superb model of a *munka*-style canoe which had fallen out of use by the mid-19th century. The *munka* style is characterised by a vertical bow that has the form of a bird's head, a flat topped raked stern and greater width across the gunwales. This model comes complete with a mast, a spar, four painted paddles and a baler.

First Nations peoples of the Pacific Northwest of North America are maritime peoples. Full-sized canoes used in trade, war and in visits for feasting are carved with precision, blessed during making and extensively painted. The paintings depict animal crests and use a formalised design system of interlocking shapes and outlines in red and black. Animal crests signify kin and clan and personify the histories and mythologies relating to ancestors and supernatural beings.

If Rae identified this canoe as Kwakwaka'wakw in style, the painting style identifies it as the work of master Haida carver and painter Charles Edenshaw (c.1839–1920). Edenshaw was from Haida Gwaii and worked across a range of media. Visiting the Museum in 2014, his great-grandson, the carver Jim Hart, recognised the flow and ingenuity of Edenshaw's hand, especially his use of space and the downturned rendering of the eyes. Hart identified the crest on the bow as an eagle.

Rae never travelled to Haida Gwaii (the Queen Charlotte Islands). He may have bought this model canoe, along with other pieces, in 1864 during a short stay in Victoria on Vancouver Island following his completion of a telegraph survey. It may also have been part of a commissioned collection sent shortly thereafter by his nephew who worked for the Hudson's Bay Company at Fort Simpson. We may never have definitive answers. However, the puzzle points us to two remarkable individuals, Rae and Edenshaw, whose entangled fortunes are materialised in this perfectly proportioned and beautifully adorned canoe.

235

Peruvian gold

The Chimor (Chimú) Empire on the north coast of Peru was expansive, lasting from AD 1000 to 1470 before it was incorporated into the Inca empire. The imperial capital was Chan Chan, which grew from humble beginnings to a crowded metropolis and artisanal centre. Chimú nobility had rights to wear and use gold objects. Among the commoners were the artisanal class: the weavers, wood sculptors and metalsmiths, with metalsmithing peaking after the conquest of the Lambayeque region to the north (1375–1400).

For many years gold items found in the Lambayeque region were identified as northern Chimú in style. However, more recent archaeological work has shown that this was the site of a distinct culture, the Sicán culture (AD 850–1375). The Sicán culture reached its height during the Middle Sicán (AD 850–1050), evident in the technological sophistication and the diversity of precious metal objects. The capital city of Middle Sicán, Batan Grande, was a religious and administrative centre, home to monumental burial mounds that were places of public and private worship. Individual graves contained lavish offerings, including gold and silver items, such as distinctive flared beakers. The quantities found suggest they were accumulated during life.

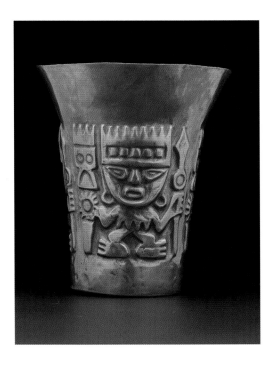

Sicán master goldsmiths organised the production of pieces which are dazzling in their artistic achievement. This flared beaker was formed over a stake using gold sheet, its low relief design created over a mould. The image is of the Sicán Lord, with upturned eyes, splayed feet, wearing a feather headdress, a tunic and large circular ear spools showing high status. Arms outstretched, he clutches two types of staff. One has a shield above the hand, and there appears to be a face with a further headdress.

Acquired in 1947, this thousand-year-old beaker was first published in 1913. It was part of the private collection of Dr James Curle, curator at the National Galleries of Scotland. Curle was brother to the archaeologist Alexander O. Curle, who was Director of the Museum.

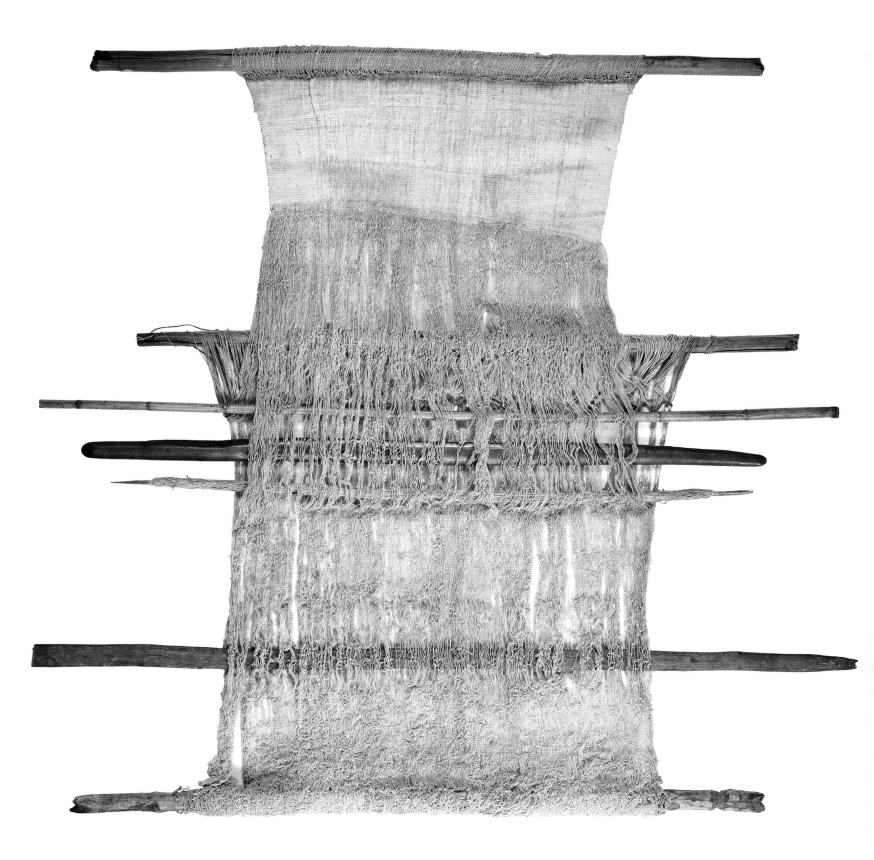

Livingstone's legacy

Scottish missionary explorer Dr David Livingstone (1813–73) travelled throughout southern and central Africa between 1841 and 1873, driven by his belief that Christianity and legitimate commerce could improve the quality of life for Africans and end the slave trade there.

In 1854, whilst Livingstone was in Africa, the Museum's first director George Wilson declared his intention to collect and display the artefacts and processes of manufacture from across the globe. In 1858 objects sent by Livingstone, an old college friend of Wilson, began to arrive at the Museum. This collection includes a weaving loom, stone mill, rocks and mineral specimens, a hippopotamus jaw, hunting net and a sample of copper wire.

In his published volumes Livingstone described in detail the extent of his travels, giving his readers the first insights into unknown and uncharted territories. In *Narrative of An Expedition to the Zambesi and Its Tributaries* (1865) his descriptions and illustrations of the type of hand-weaving loom and the grinding stone in the collection provide valuable information about these objects.

The weaving loom was collected among the Mang'anja people (in modern-day Malawi) where weaving was carried out by men using locally-grown cotton to produce a strong, long-lasting cloth. However, local weaving gradually declined in the region due to the increased availability of imported textiles. The stone mill was an essential tool for women to grind corn for cooking. Livingstone included an account of one particular woman's hard work to produce enough ground maize to exchange for a length of imported cloth. The majority of Livingstone's natural science specimens were sent to the Royal Botanic Gardens at Kew, but a large hunter's net of baobab fibre was divided and a piece sent on to this Museum. The vital role of this object in the local community is made clear in another vivid account by Livingstone, describing how zebras and antelopes were driven into these strong nets, stretched between two points.

These objects, in addition to his documented observations, reveal fascinating insights into Livingstone's concern and engagement with the people he met, and his wide-ranging interests which extended from ethnography to geography and natural sciences.

Dr David Livingstone and the stone mill, hunting net (all above) and weaving loom (opposite) that he sent to the Museum in 1858.

Ivory and salt

Carved ivories brought from west Africa to Portugal began to reach European collections at the end of the 15th century as the Portuguese opened up sea-trading networks with West Africa. Commodities including brass, iron, glass beads and firearms were exchanged for elephant ivory, gold, rubber, palm oil and slaves. A major trading partner with Europe was the kingdom of Benin in south-western Nigeria, an established and powerful empire.

The Oba, or King of Benin, controlled all trade through the kingdom and this included production of art works by his craftsmen. The major centre for the production of ivory carving was the capital of the kingdom, Benin City.

Ivory was highly valued and ivory carvings were traditionally produced only for the royal court, by craftsmen organised into a specialist guild. They worked for the Oba and required his consent to carve for other patrons. His permission was granted for production of decorated salt cellars, spoons and forks for European visitors. Ivory salt cellars were not produced for local use but only for a European market and may well have been made in workshops nearer the coastal trading ports. This was known as Bini-Portuguese ivory, acknowledging the collaboration between Benin craftsmen and European taste – in which the Bini carver produced work from drawings provided by the Portuguese.

Salt was a precious commodity in both Africa and Europe, and a highly decorated salt cellar was an item of prestige and value to be displayed in pride of place on the dining table of a wealthy European. This container is in three parts and the two spherical bowls resemble the shape of African gourds and pottery containers. The Portuguese élite are themselves the main subject of the decoration, dressed in elaborate attire. In combination with traditional Bini geometric motifs, this carving provides material evidence of the early artistic exchange between Africa and Renaissance Europe.

This object has been in the Museum collections since the 1950s, when it was purchased from a well-known London dealer of ethnographic objects.

The female spirit

This sculpture is an exceptionally fine and rare example of the skills and creativity of a specialist wood carver working in Sierra Leone in the early 19th century. The carving originates from among the neighbouring Mende or Temne people and conveys their essential ideals and characteristics of female identity at the time. Figures like this were displayed during ceremonies associated with coming of age, when young women were prepared by their elders for adult life as wives and mothers.

In a series of initiations, these girls become socialised as women and the sculpture references these changes in female identity through adornment of the body. Scarification marks on the body, the elaborate axe-shaped hairstyle and wearing of beads all identify age grades and community association. This figure is also appropriately dressed in these fitting markers of identity. From her lustrous black colour, symbolic of health and vitality, to the rings around the neck, indicating a well-fed individual, she represents a young, strong female. Her downcast eyes and closed mouth express an attitude of inner spiritual concentration and it may be that this type of figure would also have had a role in local divination societies, in ceremonies linking the world of the living with their ancestors.

The figure was collected by William Fergusson, who held the position of Governor General of Sierra Leone between 1841 and 1845. William was of mixed Scottish and Afro-Caribbean parentage, brought by his father from Jamaica as a child to be educated in Dumfries in south-west Scotland. Following medical studies in Edinburgh, he became an army surgeon in 1815, and with the Royal African Corps made his career in Sierra Leone until his death in 1846. It was during his tours of diplomatic duty that the figure was most likely acquired.

It was eventually donated to the Society of Antiquaries of Scotland in 1879 by William's son, Lieutenant Colonel Alexander Fergusson, and transferred to the Museum in 1956. Through this sculpture we not only engage with the historic traditions of carving in Sierra Leone, but also with dynamic historic connections between Scotland and this west African country.

The Angel

Created in 2008 by Gerard Quenum (b.1971), *L'Ange* is one of a series of artworks in a distinct sculptural style which addresses notions of African identity past and present.

Quenum is an artist from the Fon ethnic group, born in the coastal town of Porto Novo, the capital of the Republic of Benin. Unlike a number of successful contemporary African artists he did not train in Europe, but has developed in a tight-knit creative local environment which has led to development of an original and provocative artistic style.

His work comments on the entwined relationships between Europe and Africa through the objects he puts together. This sculpture represents not only the role of recycling for the artist, which has become synonymous with contemporary African art, but also the incorporation of objects associated with long-established beliefs and practices.

Many of Quenum's individual sculptural forms reference *bocio*, carved wooden figures which are decorated with sacred materials, including metal, beads and cloth used, by Fon priests and diviners, to provide spiritual protection for their owners. His art is given a unique twist through the use of discarded dolls which he adds to the mix of found objects. The dolls come from European aid packages sent to African children. They are collected by Quenum after they have been given up by the local street children. He transforms or 'Africanises' the dolls using a blow-torch to blacken the white skin and char the hair. By the transformation of found elements, including reclaimed wood sourced from old house frames and boat building, metalwork, shells and textiles, all with their particular histories, his sculptures are given energy and dynamism.

In this particular sculpture, a hollow container is reinvented as a body with a doll's head attached. Wings above are created from iron staffs traditionally forged by the blacksmith and once carried during local ceremonies. The base incorporates clay fragments from local pottery. As the finishing touch, Quenum pinned several small tags of red cotton to the sculpture, which he believes activate the spiritual power located within, and marks the completion of each artwork.

Bold geometry

Architecture was the leading art of the Mamluk period (1250–1517), centred on Cairo which attracted most of the building activity of the dynasty in Egypt. The Mamluk sultans, the main patrons, spent large sums on their tombs. These were usually erected adjacent to charitable complexes, which could include a mosque, theological college, hospital, and a public fountain providing drinking-water.

Highly-skilled craftsmen produced the finest fittings for these complexes. Wood was costly and used for important items such as screens, pulpits or folding lecterns. The wooden furnishings that have been preserved come mostly from religious buildings, although secular spaces, such as palaces, were probably equally embellished with intricately carved doors, window shutters, cupboards or tables.

A visually striking feature of Mamluk woodwork is inlay, with differently coloured woods, such as ebony and redwood, which are contrasted with ivory. Interwoven bands form bold geometric patterns. Only a closer view reveals the minute detail of the carved foliage enclosed in the polygonal shaped pieces.

The pattern of the large central field of this wooden panel is based on two regular twelve-pointed stars with radiating polygonal elements. They are flanked by two semi-stars and quarter-stars in the corners.

The panel is assembled from interlocking sections fitted together with tongue-and-groove jointing. This technique satisfied the taste for elaborately patterned surfaces and prevented the panels from warping.

The individual stars and polygons, which originate from the 14th century, were later set into a new redwood strapwork and frame. The ivory-inlaid ebony boards, two above and two below the central field, suggest this panel could have been used as a door. They are all carved with a single line written in the cursive *thuluth* script of the Mamluks, reading, 'Glory to God, our Lord, the Sultan, the King, the Just'.

The Museum acquired this panel from the collection of Comte de Saint-Maurice (1831–1905), a French aristocrat, who served as equerry to the Ottoman governor of Egypt.

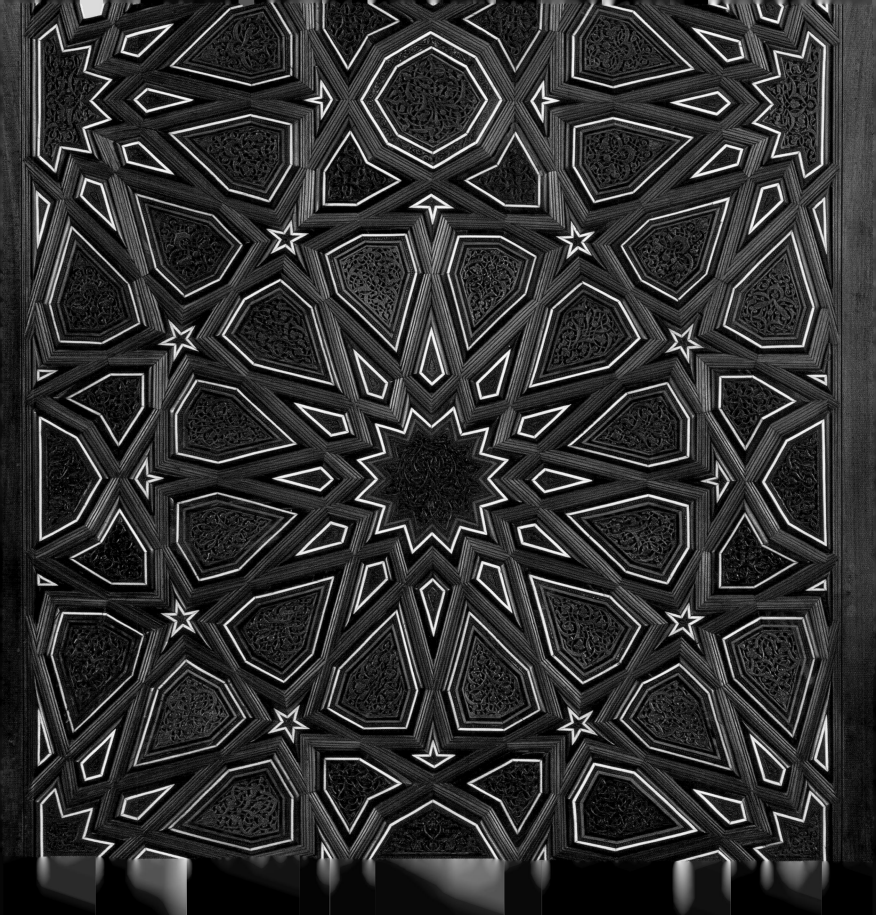

Tree of life

In the 9th to 10th centuries, under the rule of the local Samanid Dynasty, places such as Samarqand and Nishapur became centres of a flourishing cultural life. Situated in the historical region of Transoxiana and Khorasan in east Iran, and crossed by the trade routes from China to Abbasid Iraq, they benefited from an artistic exchange that is reflected in the ceramic production of this period.

Pottery was the favourite medium of artistic expression. As the large numbers of surviving vessels suggest, the glazed wares from Samarqand and Nishapur are typically slip-painted and often decorated in fine earthy pigments – dark brown and reddish ochre – which are applied on a white ground, as in this bowl dating from the 10th century. Its design consists mainly of leaf motifs, which fill the area above the two lines of pseudo Kufic script, where a tree emerges from a water jug flanked by two flower shrubs.

Craftsmen developed their own creative language. Metal-work made under the Sasanian Dynasty (AD 224–650) was one of their main sources of inspiration. The potters selected individual elements such as the palmette, a decorative motif which resembles the fan-shaped leaves of a palm tree, and embedded them into new contexts. This motif is used to create the crown of the tree and also to form the shrubs. In both shapes, the palmettes enclose brown and red painted circles, which are another motif of Sasanian origin. These 'peacock's eye' circles were used to render blossoms and the flowers of the shrubs.

The motif of a stylised tree growing from a jug probably refers to the Tree of Life, or Tree of All Seeds, mentioned in sacred texts on the origin of the universe of the ancient Iranian religion of Zoroastrianism. Plants were the fourth creation, after the sky, water and earth. They were spread all over the earth and became the source of all remedies for diseases caused by the Evil Spirit. Leaf motifs have therefore become an auspicious symbol, alluding to growth and healing as the essential properties of plants.

The Buddha

This sculpture of the seated Buddha is said to have been found near the Khyber Pass, an ancient trade route and strategic military site which connects Pakistan and Afghanistan. In the 19th century, this region was identified as the historical Gandhara. While Gandhara's geographical boundaries changed throughout time, the name has become synonymous with its artistic tradition and the Indo-Greek style of the Buddhist sculpture discovered there.

The first Buddhist missions probably reached Gandhara in the 3rd century BC. Sculptures were made to serve as cult images for sacred buildings. This statue shows chisel marks on the back that suggest it was placed in a niche against the wall.

The Buddha is depicted seated, with his legs crossed. His right hand lies above his left in his lap. This hand-gesture, or *mudra*, implies meditation (*dhyana*). The sculpture also shows some of the special bodily features which are attributes of great beings but also reflect the Buddha's spiritual power. The *nimbus* or disc behind his head represents the rays emitted by his body. The tuft of undulating hair on top of his head symbolises spirituality and his attainment of enlightenment. The raised circle (*urna*) between his eyebrows signifies spiritual insight. The long earlobes are a sign of the Buddha's secular life before enlightenment, caused by the weight of the ear ornaments he wore.

The Buddha is seated on a base which shows on its front a scene of worshippers, adoring the Buddha and the Bodhisattva, or Buddha-to-be, Maitreya.

This important sculpture was a gift from Arthur Edward Anderson (1870–1938). Although Anderson did not seem to have had a direct link to India, his father was born in Meerut, today in the state of Uttar Pradesh, where his grandfather had a business. Anderson was a connoisseur and benefactor, who donated art to many museums and galleries across the United Kingdom. Between 1927 and 1935, this Museum received more than 40 objects from him, mainly of Chinese art.

Art of the Mughal Empire

This nephrite jade dagger hilt demonstrates the high level of craftsmanship achieved at the Mughal court. The patronage of Indian hardstone carvings reached its peak during Shah Jahan's rule (1628–58), when items such as this were considered a luxury. This particular hilt probably dates from the reign of Mughal emperor Alamgir (1658–1707). It is carved in the form of a horse's head, embellished with gold and inlaid with precious stones, such as rubies and emeralds, to represent the horse's bridle and a floral design.

Daggers with hilts of precious stones were prestige items rather than weapons of war. They served as suitable vehicles for royal ostentation, particularly when attendance at court was marked by formal exchanges of gifts. The use of jade in imperial decorative art reveals the vast trade networks of the Mughal Empire and its dominance in the South Asian sub-continent. Jade and nephrite were imported from Khotan and Kashgar in Turkestan, Central Asia.

This dagger hilt was originally part of a collection of coins and precious hardstones amassed by Colonel Charles Seton Guthrie, a Scotsman who served with the Indian Army's Bengal Royal Engineers from 1828 to 1857. He probably purchased them from the Mughal and Sikh royal collections of Delhi, Lucknow and Lahore, which were being dispersed whilst he was in India. From the Museum's annual reports, it appears that Guthrie loaned parts of his collection to the Museum at various points during the late 1860s to early 1870s. The Museum then permanently acquired a number of pieces in 1875 following the auction of his collection at Christie's in London after his death.

Guthrie is representative of a large number of Scots who travelled to India, serving in the army or working as doctors, during the 18th and 19th centuries. It is thanks to these individuals the Museum has such a rich and varied collection from South Asia, connections which are maintained to this day.

Shah Akbar II (r.1806–37) in a tent, reclining on a couch with two of his sons, from India, Mughal, early 19th century.

Divine couple

This pair of carved and painted wooden figures, known as *loro blonyo* or the inseparable couple, comes from Java, Indonesia. They represent the goddess Dewi Sri and her consort Jaka Sedana. Dewi Sri is a Javanese goddess of Hindu origin. She is associated with fertility and the protection of rice fields, which are of great importance in South East Asia. Depending on local variations, status and wealth, *loro blonyo* figures were variously made from metal, terracotta or wood. The quality and style of this particular pair suggest that they may have originated from one of Central Java's 18th-century royal courts.

As well as representing the divine couple of Sri-Sedana, *loro blonyo* figures are also an imagined model for the ideal wedded couple. As a result they were used not only in ritual ceremonies associated with the rice harvest, but are also connected with marriage. The bride and groom evoke Dewi Sri and Jaka Sedana, representing hope for fertility and prosperity for themselves, just as for the rice crop.

Most Javanese houses had an inner sacred

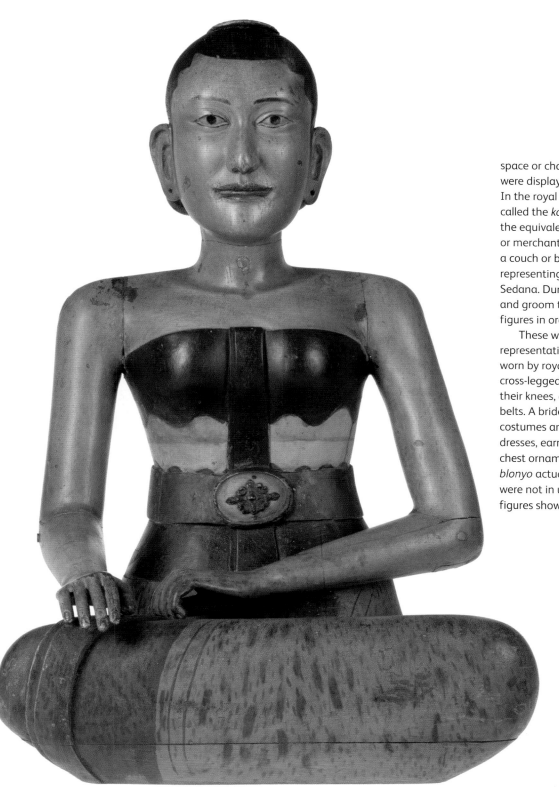

space or chamber, where the *loro blonyo* figures were displayed as part of a shrine to Dewi Sri. In the royal palaces, this inner sanctum was called the *kobongan* and was much grander than the equivalent spaces in the houses of farmers or merchants. This chamber usually contained a couch or bed, known as the *kerobongan*, representing the nuptial bed of Dewi Sri and Jaka Sedana. During wedding ceremonies, the bride and groom took the place of the *loro blonyo* figures in order to receive Dewi Sri's blessing.

These wooden figures are painted with the representation of a silk ikat textile, usually only worn by royal couples. They are carved sitting cross-legged, the folds of the cloth falling across their knees, and with elaborate buckles on their belts. A bride and groom would have worn similar costumes and been lavishly adorned with head-dresses, earrings, and gold and silver arm and chest ornaments. In some instances the *loro blonyo* actually wore the royal jewels when they were not in use, which might explain why these figures show relatively little ornamentation.

255

Indian encounters

Maharaja Duleep Singh (1838–93) was probably the first resident Sikh in Britain. Destined to rule the Sikh Empire his father Maharaja Ranjit Singh had founded, the young Maharaja lost his throne, family and fortune with the annexation of the Punjab by the British, following the Second Anglo-Sikh War of 1848–49. He became a man torn between two cultures and religions. Under the guardianship of the Scottish doctor John Login, he received a western education to prepare him for an aristocratic life in his exile in Britain. He arrived in 1854 and lived for a while in Scotland to complete his education.

This exquisitely enamelled bracelet with *makara*-headed terminals is among a group of jewellery associated with Maharaja Duleep Singh. The *makara* is a mythological creature with a fish-like body and the head of a crocodile or an elephant. Linked with different deities, it is a symbol of the creative and destructive forces of life. The open jaws of the *makara* with its rows of sharp teeth signal its fearsome character. In this bracelet the *makaras* hold a green enamelled gold mount which is set with a diamond. This perhaps refers to the strands of pearls believed to appear from their mouth as a symbol of their magnificence. Rubies were used for their eyes and tongues. The cabochon emerald on the band conceals a screw which allows the wearer to remove the *makara* heads to put on the bracelet. The bracelet's enamelled decoration echoes the colours of the gemstones. The brilliance of the translucent green, red and dark blue enamelled glass was enhanced by applying them on a high-carat gold ground. The bracelet, which is one of a pair in the Museum's collection, was probably made by Jaipur craftsmen, who were famous especially for their fiery ruby-red.

Maharaja Duleep Singh died in Paris in 1893. Later, his son Victor Duleep Singh sold parts of his inheritance at auctions, including this bracelet and further gold and silver jewellery and personal ornaments. They were bought by Major Donald Lindsay Carnegie of Spynie and Boysack (1840–1911), a Scottish numismatist or collector of coins, who bequeathed them – together with his own outstanding collection of coins – to the Museum in 1911.

Casualty of War

Casualty of War: A Portrait of Maharaja Duleep Singh is a painting by renowned British Sikh artists The Singh Twins (pictured below). It was created in 2013 as a response to pieces of jewellery in the Museum's collection that once belonged to Maharaja Duleep Singh (1838–93). Some of these ornaments were meticulously rendered by the artists in this portrait: they include the square breast pendant he is wearing on a pearl necklace, and the oblong gold pen case, enamelled bottle and silver container with bird-shaped

stopper next to his right hand. The painting highlights the jewellery's connection to one of the most important figures of British-Sikh history.

The painting shows key moments in Duleep Singh's life, first in pre-Partition India and later in Britain. By carefully combining visual elements, the artists invite the viewer to explore issues arising from his dual identity and ambivalent relationships with the British government.

Duleep Singh is depicted in all his splendour as the artists imagined him as ruler of the Sikh Empire. He wears the Sikh turban, adorned with the imperial black plume of kingship. His stately jewels include the legendary Koh-i-Noor diamond, the ultimate symbol of sovereignty and power.

The painting emphasises Duleep Singh's special relationship to his guardian, Sir John Login. Login's ambiguous role as fatherly friend and representative of British imperial interests is reflected in the chain which attaches Duleep Singh to the memorial he had erected for Login.

While still in India, Duleep Singh was educated in the faith and values of Victorian society. The objects displayed on the Kashmir shawl in front of him include, for example, an antiquarian book, which is a faithful copy of the Bible the Governor-General of India, the Earl of Dalhousie, presented to Duleep Singh on his departure from India. It symbolises the Maharaja's conversion to Christianity.

Duleep Singh finally re-converted to Sikhism. As a reminder of this, the artists added a *Khanda*, the emblem of Sikh religion, to the arched headstone of Duleep Singh's grave depicted on the right in the painting. His Christian burial at Elveden Parish Church, Suffolk, was a symbolic act by the government to ensure that his rebellion would not challenge British rule in India even after his death.

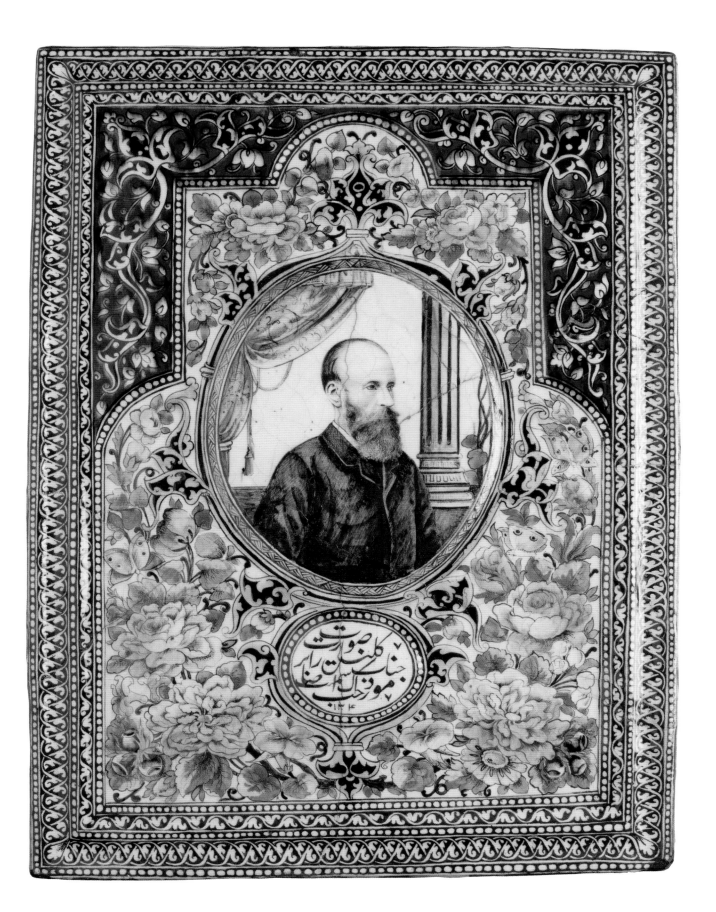

Connecting cultures

Major-General Sir Robert Murdoch Smith KCMG was a man of many skills and interests. Born in Kilmarnock in the west of Scotland in 1835, he studied natural sciences and languages at the University of Glasgow. Aged 20, he obtained a commission in the Royal Engineers. An ambitious junior officer, Murdoch Smith was selected for special employment and accompanied C T Newton, later keeper of Greek and Roman antiquities at the British Museum, on an archaeological excavation to Asia Minor.

This experience inspired him to undertake his own expedition. In 1859, he was given official permission to explore Cyrenaica and excavate at Cyrene, today in Libya. This resulted in the discovery of more than 150 classical sculptures and inscriptions, today in the collection of the British Museum.

Murdoch Smith spent the longest part of his career in Iran. In 1863, the Shah allowed Britain to build a telegraph line through Persia to connect London and Calcutta (Kolkata). Murdoch Smith was appointed superintendent and soon afterwards became director of the Persian section of the Indo-European Telegraph Department. In addition to his official duties, he volunteered to acquire Persian art for the collections of the Victoria and Albert Museum, London. The administrative skills and in-depth knowledge of Persian culture that he gained over the course of 20 years in Iran were highly valued, and in 1885 he was offered the post of Director of this Museum, the last major step in his career. He died shortly after his retirement in 1900. Murdoch Smith continued to collect and the acquisitions he made during his tenure shaped the character of the Museum's Iranian collection.

Murdoch Smith was not only a recognised authority on Iranian art; his cultural understanding was esteemed by the British government as well as the Persian court. This portrait tile was commissioned by Murdoch Smith from the Tehran master potter Ali Muhammad Isfahani when he last visited Iran on a diplomatic mission in 1887. The inscription reads 'Portrait of Colonel Robert Murdoch Smith Sahib 1304'.

When Nasir ad-Din, the Shah of Iran, toured Europe two years later, Murdoch Smith welcomed him at the Museum. The *Scotsman* newspaper reported that 'his Majesty frequently expressed his admiration for Edinburgh … [and] remarked that the Scottish people seemed to him to have shown a wonderful amount of energy not only in their own country, but wherever they went'. For this, the credit was probably due to Robert Murdoch Smith.

Robert Murdoch Smith, Director of the Museum, in 1885.

Index of objects

Jadeitite axehead

Large axehead of green Alpine jadeitite, found at Greenlawdean, Greenlaw, Berwickshire, Scotland, 3800–3000 BC.

L 248, W 105 mm
NMS X.2011.3 (pp 4–5)

Gold lunula (collar)

Found at Auchentaggart, Dumfriesshire, Scotland, probably Irish, Bronze Age, c. 2000 BC.

Diam 224 mm
NMS X.FE 3 (pp 6–7)

Carved stone ball

From Glaschul Hill, Towie, Aberdeenshire, Scotland, c. 3000 BC.

Diam 76 mm, Weight 531 g
NMS X.AS 10 (pp 8–9)

Ballachulish figure

Female figure, oak, from Ballachulish, Lochaber, The Highlands, Scotland, 750–500 BC.

H 1448 mm
NMS X.KL 54 (pp 10–11)

Four gold torcs

Blair Drummond, Perthshire, Scotland, Iron Age, found 28 September 2009.

Weight of hoard 303.49 g
NMS X.2011.6.1–4 (pp 12–13)

Acquired with the aid of the National Heritage Memorial Fund, the Art Fund (with a contribution from the Wolfson Foundation) and the Scottish Government

Hunterston brooch

Early Christian, Celtic/Anglo-Saxon style, found Hunterston, Ayrshire, Scotland. Irish or West of Scotland, AD 650–700.

Diam 122 mm
NMS X.FC 8 (pp 14–15)

Traprain hoard

Silver hoard (various), from Traprain Law, East Lothian, Scotland, AD 410–25.

Weight of hoard 22 kg
NMS X.GVA 1–176 (pp 16–17)

Cramond lioness

White sandstone, Cramond, Edinburgh, Scotland, Roman, AD 140–210, found 2009.

L 1520, W 460, D 550 mm
NMS X.1997.6 (pp 18–19)

Acquired by National Museums Scotland and City of Edinburgh Council with the aid of the Art Fund

Hilton of Cadboll stone

Cross-slab, found at Hilton of Cadboll, Ross and Cromarty, Scotland, Pictish, AD 7th/8th century,

H 2340, W 1400, D 190 mm (max)
NMS X.IB 189 (pp 20–21)

Skaill silver hoard

Viking Age silver hoard, found at Skaill Bay, Sandwick, Orkney, deposited AD 950–70.

L 140, W 200 mm (penannular brooch, above)
NMS X.IL 1–113 (pp 22–23)

Monymusk reliquary

Wooden casket and lid in form of roof, first recorded Monymusk House, Aberdeenshire, Scotland, 1859, made c. AD 700 (8th century).

H 112, L 89, W 51 mm
NMS H.KE 14 (pp 24–25)

Acquired with the aid
of the Art Fund

Lewis chessmen

Chess pieces, found in Uig, Isle of Lewis, Scotland 1831, Scandinavia, late 12th century/early 13th century.

NMS pieces: H 70–103 mm
NMS H.NS 19–29 (pp 26–27)

Bute or Bannatyne mazer

From Scotland, 1314–27, maplewood bowl with rim and straps added during 16th century.

H 110, Diam 257 mm
NMS IL.2001.182.1.1 (pp 28–29)

The Bute Collection
at Mount Stuart

Queen Mary harp

Clàrsach or Gaelic harp, made in the West Highland region, Scotland, c. 1450.

H 812, W 510, D 300 mm
NMS H.LT 1 (pp 30–31)

Penicuik jewels

Oval pendant locket of gold, enamel and seed pearl, containing portrait miniatures, Scotland, late 16th century.

H 95, W 56, D 15 mm
H.NA 422 (pp 32–33)

Penicuik jewels

Gold necklace of 14 large oval beads of filigree work divided by smaller circular beads, Scotland, late 16th century.

L 175, W 15, D 12 mm (closed)
NMS H.NA 421 (pp 32–33)

'The Maiden'

Guillotine of oak and metal, used for beheading criminals in Edinburgh, Scotland, 1564–1710.

H 1360 mm to top of blade;
base W 1530 mm
H 4000, L 3000, W 3000 mm
NMS H.MR 1 (pp 34–35)

Charles I coronation ampulla

Possibly made by James Denneistoun, deacon, Edinburgh, Scotland, 1633.

H 125, Diam 40 mm
NMS H. KJ 164 (pp 36–37)

Acquired with the aid
of the Art Fund

Louis XIII of France snaphance pistols

Pair of brass pistols, made by James Low, Dundee, Scotland, 1611.

L 356 mm (both pistols)
NMS H.LH 325, 326
(pp 38–39)

Darien chest

Iron lid and box section of safe or treasure chest of the Company of Scotland, Scotland, c. 1695.

H 660, L 1190 mm
NMS H.MJ 42, K.2000.368
(pp 40–41)

Piper to the Laird of Grant

Painting of William Cumming (c.1687–c.1723) by Richard Waitt, oil on canvas, 1714.

H 2133, L 1536 mm
NMS H.OD 69 (pp 42–43)

Charles Edward Stuart travelling canteen

Lost at the Battle of Culloden, 1746, made by Ebenezer Oliphant, Edinburgh, Scotland, hallmarked 1740–41.

H 165, W 105, D 85 mm
NMS H.MEQ 1584.1–16
(pp 44–45)

Regimental colours

Appin Stewart regimental colours carried at Culloden, Scottish Highlands, 1746.

H 1630, W 1930 mm
NMS M.1931.299.1
(pp 46–47)

Regimental colours

King's colour (Barrel Regiment) carried at Culloden, Scottish Highlands, 1746.

H 1905, W 1950 mm
NMS M.1931.299.2
(pp 46–47)

John Hynde Cotton suit in tartan

Jacket, trews and plaid (with associated leather targe), of a fine hard wool tartan, owned by Sir John Hynde Cotton, Scotland, 1744.

NMS K.2005.16.1–4
(pp 48–49)

Highland bagpipes

Acquired by Sir Joseph Noel Paton from John Francis Campbell of Islay, made by Thomas Glen, Edinburgh, c.1850.

H 1175, W 810, D 200 mm
NMS K.2001.894 (pp 50–51)

Sporran clasp with concealed pistols

Probably the model for that worn by Rob Roy in the novel *Rob Roy* by Sir Walter Scott (1818).

H 100, L 155, W 45 mm
NMS H.NE 12 (pp 52–53)

Robert Burns pistols

Double-barrelled pistols, made in Birmingham by Blair of London, England, late 18th century, owned by Robert Burns, 1788–96.

L 400, H 140 mm (both pistols)
NMS H.LH 24, 25 (pp 54–55)

Arthur's Seat coffins

Miniature coffins found on Arthur's Seat, Edinburgh, Scotland, in June 1836.

H 95, L 23, W 16 mm (coffin)
H 75, L 17, W 12 mm (figure)
NMS H.NT 86.1–8 (pp 56–57)

Daniel Laidlaw medals

Victoria Cross awarded for gallantry, Battle of Loos, 25th September 1915, to Piper Daniel Laidlaw.

H 85, W 38 mm (Victoria Cross)
NMS M.2005.68.1 (pp 58–59)

Presented by the family of the late Victor Laidlaw, son of Piper Laidlaw VC

Scottish Parliament commemorative medal

Presented to Iain Gray MSP to celebrate opening of Scottish Parliament, 1 July 1999, Royal Mint commission, 1999.

Diam 63 mm
NMS K.1999.1470.1 (pp 60–61)

By kind permission of the Royal Mint

Hamilton Rothschild tazza

Byzantine sardonyx bowl on enamelled gold foot, assembled by 10th Duke of Hamilton, early 19th century.

H 260, W 270, D 180 mm
NMS K.2012.79 (pp 66–67)

Accepted by HM Government in lieu of Inheritance Tax and allocated to National Museums Scotland, 2012

Console table

Top by Lucio de Lucci, base attrib. to Andrea Brustolon, Venice, Italy, c.1688.

H 900, W 1715, D 870 mm
NMS K.2012.26 (pp 68–69)

Acquired with the aid of the Heritage Lottery Fund, the Art Fund, the Lindsay Endowment Fund held in the National Museums Scotland Charitable Trust, the Wolfson Foundation and the Edinburgh Decorative and Fine Arts Society

Giltwood armchair

Made for Sir Lawrence Dundas, designed by Robert Adam, made by Thomas Chippendale workshop, London, 1765.

H 1048, W 760, D 755 mm
NMS K.2002.9 (pp 70–71)

Accepted by HM Government in lieu of Inheritance Tax and allocated to National Museums Scotland, 2002

Carpet known as the 'Kinghorne carpet', with monogram

English turkeywork, c.1620.

L 5300, W 2450 mm
NMS H.SO 20 (pp 72–73)

Acquired with the aid of the Art Fund

Princess Pauline Borghese travelling service

Assembled by Martin-Guillaume Biennais, Paris, France, c.1803.

H 187, W 573, D 400 mm
NMS A.1986.5.1 (pp 74–75)

Acquired with the aid of the National Heritage Memorial Fund and the Art Fund

Triumph of Prudence tapestry

Tapestry depicting the 'Triumph of Prudence', Flemish, early 16th century.

H 4100, W 5500 mm
NMS A.1898.324 (pp 76–77)

Ivory medallion and bust

Portrait of George Mackenzie, Viscount Tarbat and 1st Earl of Cromartie, and bust of John Mackenzie, 2nd Earl of Cromartie, both by David Le Marchand, Edinburgh, Scotland, late 16th century.

H 80, W 65 mm
NMS K.2015.35.1 (medallion)
NMS K.2015.34 (bust)
(pp 78–79)

Acquired with the aid of the Art Fund and the Lindsay Endowment Fund held in the National Museums Scotland Charitable Trust

Charles Rennie Mackintosh bookcase

White painted bookcase, pinewood, designed by Charles Rennie Mackintosh for Dunglass Castle, Dunbartonshire, Scotland, 1900.

H 1320, W 2930, D 320 mm
NMS H.SVB 9 (pp 80–81)

Summer

Gesso panel, by Margaret
Macdonald Mackintosh,
Glasgow, Scotland, 1904.

H 1155, W 570 mm
NMS H.SVB 4 (pp 82–83)

'Willowwood', grand piano

Case designed by Robert
Lorimer, 1909, painted by
Phoebe Anna Traquair, 1910,
piano by Steinway, wood-
carving by Scott Morton & Co.,
Edinburgh and London.

H 990, W 1440, D 2120 mm
NMS A.1995.605 (pp 84–85)

'Lago di Como' vase

Designed by Paul Perdizet
(1870–1938), manufactured
by Gallé Glass factory, Nancy,
France, c. 1920.

H 275, Circ 640 mm
NMS K.2014.75 (pp 86–87)

Teapot

Designed by Christopher
Dresser, made by James Dixon
& Sons, Sheffield, England,
c. 1879.

H 115, W 225, D 118 mm
NMS A.1994.411 (pp 88–89)

Acquired with the aid of the
National Heritage Memorial Fund
and the Art Fund

Dressing table

Dressing table, stained and
painted wood, designed by
Marcel Breuer, Dessau,
Germany, 1925.

H 1820, W 1280, D 370 mm
NMS A.1988.22 (pp 90–91)

Capra, glass sculpture

Designed by Pablo Picasso,
made by Egidio Costantini at
Fucina degli Angeli, Italy,
1954.

H 280, L 260, W 200 mm
NMS K.2015.31 (pp 92–93)

© Succession Picasso/DACS,
London 2016

Plates by Eduardo Paolozzi

Designed by Eduardo Paolozzi,
manufactured by Josiah Wedgwood and Sons Ltd, Staffordshire, England, c. 1970.

Diam 270 mm
NMS A.1998.148–153
(pp 94–95)

© Trustees of the Paolozzi
Foundation licensed by DACS 2016/
Josiah Wedgwood and Sons Ltd

Campionissimo, bowl

Inspired by 60th anniversary
of Fausto Coppi winning Giro
d'Italia and Tour de France;
designed by Drummond
Masterton, England, 2009.

H 137, Diam 247 mm
NMS K.2009.262 (pp 96–97)

© Drummond Masterton

Vase

Porcelain vase, by Lucie Rie,
England, 1974.

H 296, Diam 152 mm
NMS A.1974.234 (pp 98–99)

© Lucie Rie

Brooch

Brooch, 22-carat red gold and
niello, by Giovanni Corvaja,
Italy, 1997.

H 10, W 65, D 65 mm
NMS K.1999.418 (pp 100–1)

© Giovanni Corvaja

Emblem on red, tapestry

Tapestry designed by Graham
Sutherland, 1977, made by
Edinburgh Tapestry Company,
Scotland, 1980.

H 1685, W 1570 mm
NMS A.1981.159 (pp 102–3)

Edition 2, designed by Graham
Sutherland, woven at Dovecot
Tapestry Studio, Edinburgh, 1980

Coat dress

Dress of navy blue leather,
designed by Jean Muir,
England, 1966–95.

UK 10 dress size
L 1180, W 940 mm
NMS K.2005.649.589.1, 2
(pp 104–5)

© Jean Muir Ltd

Ankle boots

Leather and mink horseshoe
boots, designed by Sarah
Burton for Alexander
McQueen, London, England,
Autumn/Winter 2012/13.

NMS K.2014.26.1, 2 (pp 106–7)

Reproduced with permission from
Alexander McQueen

Jacket

Black velvet with metallic
embroidery, designed by Elsa
Schiaparelli, Paris, France,
Autumn/Winter 1937/38.

W 670, L 580 mm (flat)
NMS K.2014.50 (pp 108–9)

© Schiaparelli

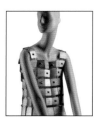

Tunic

Chain-linked armour plated
tunic, designed by Paco
Rabanne, Paris, France, 1967.

NMS K.2015.1
(pp 110–11)

© Paco Rabanne

Court mantua

Bodice and train in cream silk brocaded in gold and coloured silks, probably 1750s.

H 1430, W 2420 mm
NMS K.2013.67.1, 2
(pp 112–13)

Dufresne Collection

Collection of approximately 10,000 insects, purchased by the University of Edinburgh from Louis Dufresne (1752–1832) in 1819, later transferred to the Museum.

NMS Z.1819.2 (pp 118–19)

Beetle specimens

Five longhorn beetles, *Pogonocherus fasciculatus*; one water beetle, *Graphoderus cinereus*, in collections of William Darwin Fox and Charles Darwin, 1830s.

NMS Z.1922.13 A (pp 120–21)

Giant clam shell

Tridacna gigas, Australia, collected by Sir John Murray on HMS *Challenger* expedition (1872–76).

H 650, L 920, D 600 mm
Weight 143 kg
NMS Z.2002.156 (pp 122–23)

Giant spider crab

Macrocheira kaempferi, dried specimen.

H 1200, L 1800, D 500 mm
NMS Z.DT.409 (pp 124–25)

Giant squid tentacle club

Architeuthis dux, wet specimen, collected by Professor James Ritchie, East Lothian, Scotland, 29 October 1917.

H 615 mm (jar)
NMS Z.1917.54.1 (pp 126–27)

Westlothiana lizziae ('Lizzie') fossil

Fossil stem-amniote tetrapod, lived 345 mya, Lower Carboniferous, found by Stan Wood, East Kirkton Quarry, West Lothian, Scotland, mid-1980s.

H 34, L 186, W 120 mm
H 24, L 165, W 122 mm
NMS G.1990.72.1 (p. 128–29)

Pterichthyodes milleri fossil

Heavily armoured placoderm, Devonian (Middle Old Red Sandstone), 358–416 mya, Cromarty, Ross and Cromarty, Scotland.

NMS G.1859.33.5
NMS G.1978.50.25 (*Homostius milleri*, fossil) (pp 130–31)

Hugh Miller statue

Marble statue of Hugh Miller (1802–56), geologist and writer, examining a fossil fish, by Amelia Paton Hill, Edinburgh, 1869.

H 1210, L 520, W 440 mm
NMS A.1887.735 (pp 130–31)

Woodlouse in amber

Myanmariscus deboiseae in Burmese amber, Late Cretaceous (99 million years old), from Noije Burn, northern Myanmar.

L 3 mm (woodlouse)
NMS G.2010.20.42 (pp 132–33)

Biting midge in amber

Archiculicoides andersoni in Burmese amber, Late Cretaceous (99 million years old), from Noije Burn, northern Myanmar.

L 1 mm (biting midge)
NMS G.2010.20.24 (pp 132–33)

Earwig in amber

Haplodiplatys crightoni, in Mexican amber, Early Miocene (15–20 million years old), from Simojovel, Mexico.

L 10 mm (earwig)
NMS G.2011.31.1 (pp 132–33)

Fairy wasp and gall midge in amber

Mymaridae and Cecidomyiidae in Dominican amber, Early Miocene (16 million years old), from the Dominican Republic.

L 0.5 mm (fairy wasp)
NMS G.2013.5.10 (pp 132–33)

Rhynie Chert

Rhynie Chert containing fossil plant stems, Early Devonian (412 million years old), from Rhynie, Aberdeenshire, Scotland.

H 310, L 600, D 160 mm
NMS G.2006.6.2 (pp 134–35)

Ballarat gold nugget

Gold (bright yellow metallic crystals forming a nugget) from Ballarat, Victoria, Australia.

L 80, W 53, D 15 mm
Weight 188.6 g
NMS G.1921.2.7 (pp 136–37)

Strathmore meteorite (Keithick fragment)

Ordinary chondrite (group L, stony meteorite), intermediate olivine-hypersthene, fell 3 December 1917 at Strathmore, Perthshire, Scotland.

L 116, W 96, D 84 mm, Wt 1166 g
NMS G.1962.7 (pp 138–39)

Strontianite

Bundle of green columnar crystals, associated with baryte and brewsterite, from Whitesmith Mine, Strontian, Argyll, Scotland; acquired from Matthew Forster Heddle.

L 60, H 45 W 45 mm Wt 126.5 g
NMS G.280.13 (pp 140–41)

Lanarkite

Translucent greyishgreen bladed crystals in matrix with minor pyromorphite, Leadhills-Wanlockhead area, Scotland.

L 51, H 29, W 49 mm, Wt 77.36 g
NMS G.1995.88.1
(pp 142–43)

Susannite

Greenish-grey translucent prismatic crystals on matrix, with leadhillite, minor lanarkite and possibly macphersonite, from Leadhills, Lanarkshire, Scotland.

L 39, H 26, W 33 mm, Wt 40.07 g
NMS G.1994.128.1 (pp 142–43)

Steller's sea cow, skull

Hydrodamalis gigas, collected by Sir D'Arcy Wentworth Thompson from Copper Island, 1896–97; species extinct 18th century.

L 620, W 340, H 300 mm
NMS Z.1956.57.1 (pp 144–45)

Sperm whale, 'Moby'

Physeter macrocephalus, skeleton of adult male, Airth, near Falkirk, Scotland, 31 March 1997.

L 15.2 m
body weight 38.5 tonnes
NMS Z.1997.35 (pp 146–47)

Quagga

Equus quagga, extinct zebra lacking stripes on body; specimen from London Zoo, 1858–72.

L 828, W 610, H 1524 mm
NMS Z.1879.35.1 (pp 148–49)

Giant panda, Ching Ching

Ailuropoda melanoleuca, adult female, Ching Ching (1972–85), mounted specimen, Szechwan, China, died at London Zoo, 1985.

L 650, W 1100, H 1300 mm
NMS Z.1986.19 (pp 150–51)

Scaly-throated earthcreeper

Upucerthia dumetaria, Coquimbo, Chile, 1835, collected during Charles Darwin's voyage on HMS *Beagle* (1831–36), possibly by assistant Syms Covington.

L 190, W 140, H 137 mm
NMS Z.1931.76.10 (pp 152)

New Caledonian crow

Corvus moneduloides, female, Tendea, New Caledonia, died in captivity, 6 June 2007.

L 355, W 130, H 195 mm
NMS Z.2009.18 (crow)
Z.2011.68 (non-hooked stick tool)
(pp 153)

Dolly the sheep

Ovis aries, Finn Dorset breed, born 5 July 1996 at Roslin Institute, Midlothian, Scotland, died 14 February 2003.

H 880, L 1370, D 670 mm
NMS Z.2003.40 (pp 158–59)

Boulton and Watt beam engine

Designed by James Watt in 1786, for Barclay & Perkins Brewery, Southwark, London, England.

H 9500, L 9500, W 5000 mm
NMS T.1886.38 (pp 160–61)

Percy Pilcher *Hawk* glider

Monoplane glider built in Glasgow by Percy Sinclair Pilcher (1866–99), bamboo braced with wire and covered with fabric, 1896.

H 2057, L 5640, W 7518 mm
NMS IL.2001.222 (pp 162–63)
Royal Aeronautical Society

Freddy the robot

World's first thinking male robot to combine 'eye' and 'hand', University of Edinburgh, 1970s.

H 2500, W 3400, D 2200 mm
NMS T.1984.185 (pp 164–65)
Courtesy of
The University of Edinburgh

Wylam Dilly railway locomotive

Constructed by William Hedley, 1813; used to pull coal at Wylam Colliery, County Durham, north-east England.

L 7000, W 2200 mm
NMS T.2002.38 (pp 166–67)

**John Boyd Dunlop
pneumatic tyre**

Bicycle wheel fitted with first
pneumatic bicycle tyre,
developed by John Boyd
Dunlop, Scotland and Belfast,
1888.

H 665, W 660, D 140mm
NMS T.1910.27 (pp 168–69)

**Mike Burrows
carbon-fibre bicycle**

Fibre composite *monocoque*
frame, alloy rims, tubular tyres,
alloy profile handlebars, Mike
Burrows (b.1943), 1985.

L 1540, H 970, W 435mm
NMS T.1999.164 (pp 170–71)
By kind permission of
Mike Burrows

**Robert Wilson
demonstration piece**

Propelled by clockwork
mechanism, made by Robert
Wilson, Dunbar, Scotland,
1826.

L 845, H 255, W 272mm
NMS T.1955.11 (pp 172–73)

**Elias Howe, lockstitch
sewing machine**

One of the first six of 1846-
type machines, invented by
Elias Howe in Massachusetts,
North America.

H 335, Diam 368mm
NMS T.1935.139 (pp 174–75)

**Wilbur and Orville Wright
aeroplane engine**

Four-cylinder Wright aeroplane engine, built in
1910, fitted to a
Wright Model B Airplane,
gifted by Orville Wright.

L 990, H 730, W 360mm
NMS T.1927.26 (pp 176–77)

**Colonel Henry Holden
motor bicycle**

Motor bicycle with four-
cylinder engine, built by
Colonel Sir Henry Capel Lofft
Holden, 1895.

H 980, L 1530, W 565mm
NMS T.1922.113 (pp 178–79)

**John Logie Baird
Televisor**

30-line television receiver,
1930, invented by John Logie
Baird (1888–1946).

H 300, W 465, D 285mm
NMS T.1963.48 (pp 180–81)

**EMAS
prosthetic arm**

EMAS (Edinburgh Modular
Arm System), Edinburgh,
1998.

L 750, W 220, 100mm
NMS T.2010.120 (pp 182–83)

**i-Limb
prosthetic hand**

Original model, Touch Bionics,
Livingston, 2008.

H 185, D 60, W 80mm
NMS T.2012.18 (pp 182–83)
From Touch Bionics

**Five-needle
telegraph instrument**

With rhombus-shaped
keyboard.

H 1165, W 660, D 75mm
NMS IL.2016.7.8 (pp 184–85)
King's College, London

**CERN copper
accelerating cavity**

Accelerating cavity from
CERN's Large Electron-
Positron Collider (LEP),
operational 1989–2000.

H 2500, W 1000, D 2000mm
NMS T.2014.34 (pp 186–87)
Donation by CERN

**'Mouse box' prototype
for MRI scanner**

For Magnetic Resonance
Imager (MRI), designed by
Professor John Mallard and
research group at University
of Aberdeen, 1974.

H 111, Diam 254mm
NMS T.2006.13 (pp 188–89)

Sir James Black medals

Group of medals (including
the Nobel medal 1988),
awarded to Professor James
Black, pharmacologist.

Nobel medal Diam 68, D 3mm
NMS IL.2009.2
On loan from Rona Mackie Black,
widow of Sir James Black

Other medals:
NMS T.2009.60.1,
T.2009.60.21.1, T.2009.60.56.1,
T.2009.60.68.1, T.2009.60.99.1,
T.2009.60.101.1, T.2009.233.1
Molecular model (propranolol)
NMS D.2011.6
Supplied by Miramodus Ltd
www.miramodus.com
(all on pp 190–91)

**W H Fox Talbot
photographic equipment**

Calotype camera, *c.* 1840,
used by W H Fox Talbot,
inventor of photographic
negative/positive process.

H 250, W 245, D 210mm
NMS T.1936.21 (pp 192–93)

Joseph Black laboratory equipment

Cucurbit or solution glass, used in lectures 1766–99, possibly made in glassworks, Edinburgh, Scotland.

NMS T.1858.275
(pp 194–95)

Cod-head isolator

An isolator switch, 1930, used at Portobello Substation, Edinburgh, Scotland.

H 2680, W 3420, D 440mm
NMS T.1990.47.2 (pp 196–97)

Triple expansion engine, model

Model of engine for ocean steamers *Zealandia* and *Australia*, from drawings by original makers Elder & Co., Glasgow.

H 110, D 950, W 700mm
NMS T.1879.60 (pp 198–99)

Qurna coffin

Excavated in 1908 by Sir W M Flinders Petrie (1853–1942), at Sheikh Abd el-Qurna, Egypt, from 17th Dynasty (c.1585–45 BC).

H 165, L 2060, W 470mm
NMS A.1909.527.1 and A
(pp 204–5)

Funerary canopy

Excavated by Alexander Henry Rhind (1833–63), canopy made for Montsuef, at Sheikh Abd el-Qurna, Egypt, 9 BC (Early Roman Period).

H 840, L 2110, W 865mm
NMS A.1956.353
(pp 206–7)

Limestone wall panel

Relief from the palace of Assyrian King Ashurnasirpal II (883–59 BC), Nimrud, Iraq, which once belonged to the doctor Sir James Young Simpson (1811–70).

H 2413, W 2184mm
NMS A.1956.362 (pp 208–9)

Ancient Greek *lekythos*

Lekythos (oil vase) with black-figure decoration on white-ground; name vase of 'The Edinburgh Painter', Attic, ancient Greece, c.500 BC.

H 305mm
NMS A.1956.436 (pp 210–11)

Miyamoto Musashi battling the giant whale

Woodblock triptych print by Utagawa Kuniyoshi (1797–1861), Japan, 1848.

H 368, W 754mm
NMS A.1887.745.68.4.43–45
(pp 212–13)

Water jar for tea ceremony

Porcelain with underglaze blue decoration, made in Hirado Mikawachi, Japan, 1780–1880.

H 242mm
NMS V.2015.10.36 (pp 214–15)

Presented by David and Ann Hyatt King through the Art Fund

Imperial rice measure

Carved polychrome lacquered wood, China, Jiajing reign (AD 1521–67), Ming Dynasty.

H 163, L 322, W 322mm
NMS A.1930.496 (pp 216–17)

Imperial seat (*dabaozou*)

Black lacquered wood, decorated in gold, China, Qing Dynasty, 18th century.

H 1030, L 1300, W 865mm
NMS A.1950.176 (pp 218–19)

Imperial concubine's Semi-formal dragon robe

Illustrations in *Regulations for Ceremonial Paraphernalia of the Qing Dynasty* (*Huangchao liqi tushi*), ink/colours on silk, China, Qing Dynasty, 1759.

H 421, W 409mm
NMS A.1968.432 S (dragon robe)
A.1968.432 F (pp 220–21)

Large fish bowl

Porcelain with overglaze polychrome enamels made at Jingdezhen, China, Longqing reign (1567–72), Ming Dynasty.

H 350, Diam 550mm
NMS A.1919.406 (pp 222–23)

Lotus-shaped cup and stand

Stoneware with celadon glaze and inlaid underglaze designs, Korea, Goryeo Dynasty, AD 918–1392.

H 75, Diam 140mm
NMS A.1919.496 (pp 224–25)

Maori war canoe

Waka taua, Bay of Plenty, New Zealand, pre-1827, wood, incorporating acrylic stern post, by George Nuku, 2008.

L 5700, H 1620, D 500mm
NMS A.UC.767 (canoe),
V.2008.96 (stern post)
(pp 226–27)

Stern post © George Nuku

Gorget

Cane with feathers, dog hair, shark teeth, pearl-shell and fibre, Tahiti, Society Islands, 18th century, collected in 1778 on Captain James Cook's third voyage to Pacific.

H 440, W 610 mm
NMS A.1956.1025 (p. 228–29)

Ceremonial bowl

Admiralty Islands, Papua New Guinea, 19th century, given to Society of Antiquaries of Scotland, 1901, by John Young Buchanan, HMS *Challenger* Expedition (1872–76).

H 520, W 1030, D 720 mm
NMS A.1956.864 (pp 230–31)

Carved effigy club

Ball-headed club of alder wood, painted, with wool and feathers, probably Haudenosaunee (Iroquois), Canada, 1847–54.

L 650, W 80 mm
NMS A.1989.208 (pp 232–33)

Model canoe, *munka*-style

Painted wood, Kwaw̲aka̲'wakw and Haida, British Columbia, Canada, 1860s–80s.

L 980, W 210, H 250 mm
NMS A.L.304.109 and A–G
(pp 234–35)

Courtesy of
The University of Edinburgh

Sicán gold beaker

Decorated with repoussé design, Sicán culture, La Merced, Lambayeque Valley, Peru, 9th–11th century.

H 120, Diam 100 mm
NMS A.1947.170 (pp 236–37)

Weaving loom

Hand loom of wood and cane, with woven cotton sample, Mang'anja people, Mozambique or Malawi, southern Africa, collected late 1850s.

L 1400, W 1170 mm
NMS A.762.2 (pp 238–39)

Hand mill

Grinding stone in two parts, Mang'anja people, Lower Shire River Valley, Malawi, southern Africa, collected late 1850s.

L 430, Diam 178 mm
NMS A.762.1 (pp 238–39)

Hunter's net

Net of baobab fibre, southern Africa, collected late 1850s.

L 4880, W 1830 mm
NMS A.594
(pp 238–39)

Salt-cellar

Container of carved elephant ivory in three parts, Bini people, Benin, Nigeria, West Africa, 16th century.

H 210, W 90 mm
NMS A.1950.3 A, B (pp 240–41)

Carved female figure

Sculpture of wood with glass beads and metal parts, Temne or Mende people, Sierra Leone, West Africa, collected *c.* 1843.

H 584, W 110 mm
NMS A.1956.1159 (pp 242–43)

L'Ange (Angel)

Sculpture of wood, with metal, clay, textile and plastic, by Gerard Quenum, Fon people, Porto Novo, Republic of Benin, West Africa, 2008.

H 2300, W 300 mm
NMS V.2009.212 (pp 244–45)

© Gerard Quenum

Wooden panel

With geometric decoration, carved and inlaid with ebony and ivory, Egypt, 14th century.

H 2718, W 1213 mm
NMS A.1884.2.1 (pp 246–47)

Earthenware bowl

Slip-painted earthenware, decorated with foliate ornament and Kufic calligraphy, Eastern Iran, 10th century.

H 83, D 258 mm
NMS A.1976.317 (pp 248–49)

Buddha sculpture, meditating

Sculpture of the Buddha in *dhyana mudra*, grey schist, Gandhara, 2nd–3rd century.

H 1150, W 650, D 320 mm
NMS A.1933.155 (pp 250–51)

Dagger hilt

In the shape of a horse's head, light green jade inlaid with gold and precious stones, India, Mughal, 17th century.

L 125 mm
NMS A.1875.29.4 (pp 252–53)

271

**Bridal couple
(loro blonyo)**

Figures of a bride and groom,
representing the goddess
Dewi Sri and her consort,
carved and painted wood,
Java, probably 18th century.

H 525, W 330 mm
NMS A.1991.65 A, B (pp 254–55)

Bracelets

Pair of bracelets with *makara*-
headed terminals, gold,
enamelled and set with
precious stones, associated
with Maharaja Duleep Singh,
Northern India, 1800–50.

Diam 85 mm
NMS A.1911.453 and 454
(pp 256–57)

***Casualty of War: A Portrait
of Maharaja Duleep Singh***

Painting in miniature style
with a portrait of Maharaja
Duleep Singh (1838–93),
watercolour, poster paint, gold
dust on mount board, by The
Singh Twins, England, 2013.

H 495, W 455 mm
NMS V.2013.31 (pp 258–59)

Acquired with aid from
British Council Scotland

© The Singh Twins
www.singhtwins.co.uk

Wall tile

With portrait of Robert
Murdoch Smith (1835–1900),
polychrome underglaze
painted tile by Ali Muhammad
Isfahani, Tehran, Iran, 1887.

H 500, W 350 mm
NMS IL.2009.14 (pp 260–61)

On loan from a private lender

Acknowledgements

Pages 12–13 Four gold torcs: Acquired with the aid of the National Heritage Memorial Fund, the Art Fund (with a contribution from the Wolfson Foundation) and the Scottish Government; 18–19 Cramond lioness: Acquired by National Museums Scotland and City of Edinburgh Council with the aid of the Art Fund; 24–25 Monymusk reliquary: Acquired with the Aid of the Art Fund; 28–29 Bute or Bannatyne mazer: The Bute Collection at Mount Stuart; 36–37 Charles I coronation ampulla: Acquired with the aid of the Art Fund; 58–59 Daniel Laidlaw medals: Presented by the family of the late Victor Laidlaw, son of Piper Laidlaw VC; 60–61 Scottish Parliament commemorative medal: By kind permission of the Royal Mint; 66–67 Hamilton Rothschild tazza: Accepted by HM Government in lieu of Inheritance Tax and allocated to National Museums Scotland, 2012; 68–69 Console table: Acquired with the aid of the Heritage Lottery Fund, the Art Fund, the Lindsay Endowment Fund held in the National Museums Scotland Charitable Trust, the Wolfson Foundation and the Edinburgh Decorative and Fine Arts Society; 70–71 Giltwood armchair: Accepted by HM Government in lieu of Inheritance Tax and allocated to National Museums Scotland, 2002; 72–73 'Kinghorne carpet': Acquired with the aid of the Art Fund; 74–75 Princess Pauline Borghese travelling service: Acquired with the aid of the National Heritage Memorial Fund and the Art Fund; 78–79 Ivory medallions and bust: Acquired with the aid of the Art Fund and the Lindsay Endowment Fund held in the National Museums Scotland Charitable Trust; 88–89 Christopher Dresser teapot: Acquired with the aid of the National Heritage Memorial Fund and the Art Fund; 92–93 *Capra* glass sculpture © Succession Picasso/DACS, London 2016; 94–95 Eduardo Paolozzi plates © Trustees of the Paolozzi Foundation licensed by DACS 2016/Josiah Wedgwood and Sons Ltd; 96–97 *Campionissimo* bowl © Drummond Masterton; 98–99 Vase © Lucie Rie; 100–1 Brooch © Giovanni Corvaja; 102–3 *Emblem on Red*, tapestry: Edition 2, designed by Graham Sutherland, woven at Dovecot Tapestry Studio, Edinburgh, 1989; 104–5 Coat dress © Jean Muir Ltd; 106–7 Leather and mink horseshoe boots: Reproduced with permission from Alexander McQueen; 108–9 Velvet jacket © Schiaparelli; 110–11 Tunic © Paco Rabanne; 162–63 Percy Pilcher *Hawk* glider: Royal Aeronautical Society; 164–65 Freddy the Robot: Courtesy of The University of Edinburgh; 170–71 Carbon-fibre bicycle: By kind permission of Mike Burrows; 182–83 i-Limb prosthetic hand: From Touch Bionics; 184–85 Five-needle telegraph instrument: King's College, London; 186–87 CERN copper accelerating cavity: Donation by CERN; 190–91 James Black's Nobel Medal, on loan from Rona Mackie Black, widow of Sir James Black; 190–91 Molecular model for propranolol, supplied by Miramodus Ltd, www.miramodus.com; 214–15 Water jar for tea ceremony, presented by David and Ann Hyatt King through the Art Fund; 226–27 Stern post © George Nuku; 234–35 Model canoe, *Munka*-style: Courtesy of The University of Edinburgh; 244–45 *L'Ange (Angel)* © Gerard Quenum; 258–59 *Casualty of War: A Portrait of Maharaja Duleep Singh* © The Singh Twins, www.singhtwins.co.uk; 260–61 Wall tile (with portrait of Robert Murdoch Smith): On loan from a private lender.

ArtFund

With many thanks to the curators, conservators, photographers, picture library and publishing staff, collections services, and administrative staff of National Museums Scotland who have contributed to this book.

IMAGE ACKNOWLEDGEMENTS

While every effort has been made to acknowledge correct copyright of images where applicable, any unintentional omissions or errors should be notified to the Publisher, who will arrange for corrections to appear in subsequent editions.

Pages 36–37 Charles I visiting Scotland, image Royal Collection Trust/© Her Majesty Queen Elizabeth II 2016; 58–59 Piper Laidlaw, image © private collection; 70–71 Robert Adam by George Willison, image © National Portrait Gallery, London; 88–89 Christopher Dresser, image by permission of the Linnean Society of London; 90–91 Marcel Breuer, image © Anonymous/Hutton Archive/Getty Images; 120–21 Charles Darwin, Howarth-Loomes Collection at National Museums Scotland; 148–49 Quagga at London Zoo, image © The Zoological Society of London; 150–51 Ching Ching at London Zoo, image © Colin Davey/Hutton Archive/Getty Images; 176–77 Wright brothers, image © Library of Congress/Science Faction/Getty Images; 180–81 John Logie Baird, image © National Portrait Gallery, London; 204–5 Qurna coffin image, courtesy of the Petrie Museum of Egyptian Archaeology, UCL; 258–59 Singh Twins, image © The Singh Twins, www.singhtwins.co.uk.

Other images in publication © National Museums Scotland 2016 (unless otherwise credited)